INTERPRETATION
IN PIANO STUDY

INTERPRETATION
IN PIANO STUDY

JOAN LAST

LONDON
OXFORD UNIVERSITY PRESS
NEW YORK TORONTO

Oxford University Press, Ely House, London W.1

GLASGOW   NEW YORK   TORONTO   MELBOURNE   WELLINGTON
CAPE TOWN   IBADAN   NAIROBI   DAR ES SALAAM   LUSAKA   ADDIS ABABA
DELHI   BOMBAY   CALCUTTA   MADRAS   KARACHI   LAHORE   DACCA
KUALA LUMPUR   SINGAPORE   HONG KONG   TOKYO

ISBN 0 19 318411 7

© Oxford University Press 1960

First published 1960
Reprinted 1962, 1967, 1970, and 1975

Printed in Great Britain by
Fletcher & Son Ltd, Norwich

DEDICATED TO PETER KATIN

without whose encouragement this book
would never have been finished

PREFACE

There is little I can add to a book so closely concerned as this with the application of commonsense to piano-playing, except to say that I feel highly privileged to be writing its preface.

What kind of commonsense exactly? Many people can learn to put down the right keys at the right time. That involves one kind of commonsense. But the matter should not rest there, for technical ability of this sort is a means to an end and not the end itself, and it is on such a basis that Joan Last has written this brilliant and most enlightening book.

When the time is ripe for the amalgamation of matters relevant to a musical performance, many important factors are often ignored. At this critical stage, the arrival at which depends on the rate of progress and individual intelligence, much harm can be done. In some cases it is not even realized that phrasing, pedalling, tone-control, etc., are not things to be thought of as separate entities, but are factors essential to the performance of a piece of music. And, alas, the full exploration of their possibilities is all too often superficial.

Finally, while everyone surely knows that musicianship is largely a matter of using one's ears, it is not enough to leave it at that—the question is *how* to use them. If I am told 'listen', I have no idea if I am to listen to a bird, distant thunder, or the doorbell. And so the pianist must know what to listen for. But he must also be made aware of the fact that what he hears is capable, at his hands, of infinite shaping towards the moment when he can truthfully say, 'I *know* that piece'.

PETER KATIN

CONTENTS

ACKNOWLEDGEMENTS

I should like to thank all my friends and pupils who have contributed in so many ways towards the preparation of this book. I am also greatly indebted to Rosalyn Tureck for invaluable advice on the sections relating to the music of Bach.

Thanks are also due to Augener Ltd. for permission to quote from Gabriel Grovlez's 'Chanson d'escarpolette' from *L'Almanach aux images*; to MM. Durand & Cie., Paris, for permission to quote from Debussy's 'Arabesque No. 1', 'La Cathédrale engloutie', and 'Dr. Gradus ad Parnassum'; and to Editions Jean Jobert, Paris, for permission to quote from Debussy's 'Clair de Lune' (sole agents for these Debussy works: United Music Publishers Ltd.).

J. L.

AUTHOR'S FOREWORD

In part of the Foreword to my earlier book, *The Young Pianist*, I put forward the idea that there is a degree of attainment which can be reached in every grade of piano-playing, from the lowest to the highest. Suggestions towards this ideal were made in Part III of the book, and it is the ideas there set out that I now hope to expand, adding others that may help or guide the student who has left the beginner stages behind.

It must be realized that *grade* and *standard* in piano-playing are not one and the same thing, and it is a sad fact that, as the student passes through the grades, his standard often becomes lower. The further the aspiring pianist progresses the more it should become apparent to him that a good performance involves infinitely more than simply pushing down the right keys at the right moment. There are many who protest that they only play 'for the fun of it', but I am sure that these people too will get far more fun from their music-making if the results are pleasant to listen to.

Interpretation is more concerned with *sounds* than it is with *notes*; thus our first aim in 'giving a performance' is to produce the *kind of sound* that the musical context demands. In assessing quality and quantity of tone, one must always consider the note that has gone before and that which is to follow. Here the pianist has to contend with the limitations of the individual instrument. It is thus more than ever important that he should develop a sensitivity of ear and finger, so that he can gauge the possibilities of touch and tone in their varying qualities.

To the serious student the production of tone involves an understanding of the conditions required in the arms, hands, and fingers. Books and books have been written on the subject, which is, indeed, a most important part of the pianist's training. I sometimes feel, however, that in this maze of technical fact the core of the whole thing is nearly forgotten— that is, the necessity for a 'listening desire' which communicates itself to the arms, hands, and fingers. I would call this 'musical intention'. Of what use is it to be the master of a fine technique if there is no desire or purpose behind it? One might as well train as a long-distance walker only to go out and walk in aimless circles. The untrained athlete who sees a mountain and makes up his mind to reach the top, goes into training so that his purpose may be achieved. Similarly, the pianist with a definite artistic desire needs to study and practise technique in order to fulfil it. But the technique will have been the *servant* of the music, and not its *master*.

During the time that I have been writing this book, several people have asked me: 'To whom is it addressed, the student or the teacher?' My answer has been: 'It is addressed to both.' From experience I have found that many teachers who have excellent results with beginners do not seem to be able to maintain such a high standard with their pupils in the higher grades. This is, I feel, because they have not realized how much of the interpretative side of piano-playing has to be *taught*. The ability to interpret music is not just a heaven-sent gift, though pupils may vary considerably in their potential artistry. Even the most promising need careful guidance and teaching in the understanding of the basic principles that lie behind the art of interpretation. The less bright pupil, too, can add considerably to the value of his performance, if such principles have been instilled by the teacher.

We are all students at heart, and whether we are learning to play, teach, or write there is always something new for us to discover. I have made endless discoveries through the difficulties of my own pupils, and I feel that I should thank each one who has brought me a new problem with which to contend.

These problems form the subject-matter of this book, and

the suggestions which I have made as to their possible solution may be modified or augmented according to the experience of the reader.

We cannot apply strict methods and unbreakable rules where interpretation is concerned, and this book simply represents the experience of one of thousands of ordinary music teachers. As such it is offered to all who are interested in piano-playing.

THE MELODIC LINE

Far too many pianists do not listen critically to their own playing, yet have the ability to criticize others. It is most important to acquire the habit of self-criticism, and for this one needs to have a clear idea *why* a certain phrase sounds better played in one way than another. There can of course be differences of opinion, even between artists of integrity, but these are of a more subtle nature and do not directly concern the main structure of music.

What we must seek to attain is control of tone, both in quality and quantity, and ability to assess the relative tonal value between one note and another within the phrase. The biggest disadvantage is that *it is too easy to produce a sound on the piano!* A child of two or three will stand at the keyboard and produce excruciating sounds which can be no proof at all that he is a future virtuoso; if, at five or six, he succeeds in 'playing a tune', then his parents will probably think that he is a budding genius!

In the case of wind or stringed instruments, and even the voice, it is quite a different thing. Every note has to be produced by an accurately judged effort on the part of the performer. The beginner on a wind instrument will consider he has scored a success if he makes a sound at all! The string player has the problem of correct intonation as well as control of the bow. The five-year-old who plays a tune on the violin or flute has indeed achieved something.

These instrumentalists have to *listen to every sound they produce.* So, too, should the pianist; but unfortunately this is seldom realized.

If one speaks of a pianist as having a 'good technique' the general impression given is that he can play all the notes, however fast the tempo, and however difficult the work may be. Music is described as technically difficult if its performance demands agility or strength. It is not always realized that it requires a considerable amount of technical control to produce a cantabile touch in soft passages, or to grade a crescendo perfectly throughout a phrase. There are, of course, differences in these technical problems: speed and strength can be attained only through physical discipline of the arms, hands, and fingers, whereas tonal control is largely attained through mental discipline in which the ear and finger are completely attuned.

This tonal control is an essential part of what is called the 'expression' of music. I often think that the term 'putting in the expression' is unsuitable. One can't *put in* the expression; it is there within the music and was part of its conception. I would much prefer the term 'bringing out the expression'. Indeed, what often happens is that the expression is *taken out* by the insensitivity of the pianist, or else exaggerated effects are imposed on the music by one who wishes to make an impression upon the listener. Taste in such matters is inborn in the potential artist but can be fully developed only through experience and the understanding of certain guiding factors.

It is sometimes thought that, as the composer (or editor) has written marks of expression in the music, all one has to do is to follow them. But no mark of expression can convey fully the tonal range of a phrase; it can only indicate a general level around which there must be a rise and fall of tone, however slight.

We start, then, by considering the tonal nuance in a simple melodic line, for in this we have the foundation of what is to come. The first consideration, and one that is only too readily understood, is the *time* in which the music is written. I use the words 'only too readily' because a conscious effort to convey the natural accent of every bar would kill the rhythmic impulse of the whole. One is reminded of certain dancing classes where the teacher's '*one*, two, three, *one*, two, three' seems to defy any fluidity of movement on the part of the pupils, though it appears to be essential in their early training.

In the case of the pianist this monotonous accentuation is seldom desirable, for though rise and fall of tone is partly governed by the time of the music, it is also dependent on the 'shape' of each phrase and its point of climax. This can be more easily appreciated if the phrase is thought of as a line of song, and, however limited our vocal powers, we can discover a great deal about the shape of a phrase if we sing it. Even if we do not sing aloud we should constantly be singing inwardly as we play, for instinct in such matters is often more readily conveyed by the voice than the fingers, particularly in the case of the young student whose fingers are not yet wholly responsive or sensitive.

Let us take, as an example, a simple tune in 3/4 time:

If this is played with an equal accent on *each* first beat the music becomes stilted and all forward impulse is lost. If, however, it is considered as two short phrases of vocal line it emerges something like this:

We now realize that the last note of each phrase is soft, *even though it falls on the first beat of a bar.* Thus we learn to think and read our music in phrases rather than in bars. This applies particularly to the poor sight-reader, who often spells out each bar as a separate unit. It is essential to good sight-reading that the eye and ear should take in a phrase at a glance, and anyone who finds difficulty in doing this should practise reading a simple melodic line, looking at one complete phrase for two or three seconds, and then playing it from memory. This process is built up until the student can do the same with a phrase containing two, three, or more voices.

The pianist with a natural feeling for line, and whose rhythmic awareness is strongly developed, will not need to be told these things as far as his own performance is concerned. But as a teacher or student he needs to be able to *analyse* the difference between varying performances, and to explain why, if two people play the same phrase at the same tempo, both with correct notes and time, one may be full of vitality and the other dead and dull.

As a basis for such an analysis the student must be aware of the strong and indissoluble relationship between tonal gradation and rhythmic structure. This can, in its simplest form, be reduced to a relationship between tonal *quantity* and time values. For example, it will be noticed by anyone who sings or plays the two little phrases just quoted, that there is a natural tendency to soften the crotchet where the rhythm is

♩ ♩ This softening of the shorter note values is instinctive in those who are sensitive, but sometimes has to be pointed out to pianists who are more concerned with playing the right notes than making the right sounds. Indeed, as Geoffrey Tankard has said: 'Piano-playing is largely an art of gradation, and a teacher should teach it as carefully as he teaches legato.'[1]

There is much in music that is akin to language, and the gradation of tone in a melodic line is comparable with the rise and fall of the voice. Where words and music go hand in hand we can assess the tonal gradation of the melodic line by first *speaking* the words. In the following simple and typical examples the softened notes are in smaller type, corresponding with the softer syllables in the spoken words:

Ex. 2.   Girls and boys come out   to   play

[1] *Pianoforte Diplomas* (Elkin).

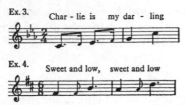

The connection between tonal quantity and time values is, indeed, so strong that wrongly stressed notes can give an impression of faulty time. I give here two examples (5 and 6) with, immediately below each (5a and 6a), the impression gained if the shorter notes are not softened:[1]

An understanding of the relationship between words and rhythmic pattern is often required of candidates in their rudiments examinations. In these the student is asked to set certain words to suitable rhythms. The test presents little difficulty if the words are chanted in a 'sing-song' manner, after which an accent is written over each stressed syllable. A bar line is then placed *before* each accent:

$$\overset{>}{\text{O}}\text{ver the } | \overset{>}{\text{hills}} \text{ and } | \overset{>}{\text{far}} \text{ a} | \overset{>}{\text{way}}$$

from this stage it should be easy to insert time signature and note values.

[1] A good Example is the Gigue from Bach's English Suite in C minor.

It may be, however, that the first accented syllable does not fall on the first word of the rhyme: this is again revealed by a sing-song method of reciting the words:

Here's a | health unto his | majesty

In *singing* the phrase this is usually made clear, but pianists often fail to realize that, where a piece of music does not begin on the first beat of the bar, its true rhythmic structure can only be conveyed to the listener *by the manner of its performance.* The pianist who stresses the first *note* instead of the first *strong beat* is conveying a faulty impression. He should learn to play the notes of the anacrusis in such a way that the gradation of tone is *towards* the strong beat. Thus the true rhythmic impulse is shown in opening phrases such as these:

Ex. 7.   Beethoven

Ex. 8.   Mozart
etc.

Finally we realize that each phrase having its own shape and point of climax, the smaller gradations of tone between one note and another serve to bring life and rhythmic impulse to the whole.

In piano music, however, the building of the complete structure includes many problems beyond those of the simple melodic line, and this chapter becomes a starting point from which to review the many aspects of tonal control as they affect individual performance.

THE FADING SOUND

As I write I realize how difficult it is going to be to divide the problems of piano-playing into sections. It is like trying to dissect and analyse a fine piece of architecture in which each part has true significance only when considered in relationship with the whole. We cannot visualize the arch without the columns that support it, nor the fine carvings without the doorway over which they appear. Yet here am I striving to do exactly that! It must be apparent, then, that much that is written in each chapter will have a bearing on what has already been said and on what is to follow. Indeed, there will be an inevitable overlapping of all sections of this book.

In the previous chapter I stressed the relationship between rhythmic structure and tonal gradation in its simplest aspect—that of the melodic line. The examples given could apply to any instrument, or to the voice. Now we must consider our own particular instrument, the piano. Here we discover one essential difference between song and piano tone. In playing the piano *the sound begins to fade immediately after the note has been struck*, and not even the use of the sustaining pedal can prevent its fading. In this the pianist faces a problem which does not beset the performer on any other instrument, and he must learn to use this condition to enhance rather than detract from his performance. It has been said that the piano is the most unmusical of instruments, but such a saying reflects on the performer rather than the instrument, and is due to the fact that, as I have already said, it is far too easy to make some kind of sound on the piano.

The fading of the sound is thus something which cannot be ignored: it must be understood and used skilfully, so that progression from one sound to another is perfectly balanced.

As a preliminary experiment let us play the two chords 6/4 5/3. Here we have a positive, or strong, harmony merging into a weaker one. It is generally recognized that the weaker of these two chords should be the softer—but how much softer? This is where judgement of the sustaining qualities of the particular instrument is necessary. Because the pianist cannot carry his own instrument around with him, he needs to be doubly sensitive to the moment when the sound is made and the speed with which it fades. Whatever the condition of the instrument the softness of the second chord depends on the speed with which the first has faded. Added to this, and of great importance too, we have to take into consideration the tempo and note values of the two sounds. The following will illustrate the point:

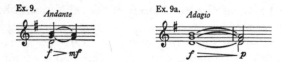

Where the music is marked 'Andante' and the progress is in crotchets the tone has very little time to fade, and so the 5/3 chord should be only a fraction softer than the 6/4. If, however, the tempo is 'Adagio' and the first chord a semibreve, the second one should be considerably softer to match the fading of the tone of the first. In fact the greater the length of the first chord the softer its resolution.

At the slow speed, were the second chord to be played at the *same* level, it would sound *louder* than the first! Let the reader experiment and discover for himself. A good visual idea of this principle can be gained by this simple diagram:

Obviously this is only the basis on which to work, for other factors in the music will inevitably condition the exact choice of tonal relationship.

As the student's listening faculty is developed he will, at first, be *consciously* directing the fingers in tonal gradation. But, in the same way that a learner driving a car thinks separately of each action required to start, accelerate, stop, and so on, until eventually the actions become one with the intention of the driver, so in the end do the fingers automatically respond to the intention of the pianist. *But there must always be an active musical intention behind each sound.*

I suggested earlier that to feel the 'shape' of a phrase one should sing it. The voice, however, having fuller sustaining qualities, cannot exactly express tonal nuances as they would sound on the piano. If the following were sung (at a suitable pitch) and then played on the piano, the difference should be easily detected:

Ex. 11. Chopin

In the sung version the longer sound 𝄐 is sustained at an even level of tone, and the quavers that follow it maintain that level. On the piano the long G will start to fade immediately after it has been struck, and were the quavers to be given the same amount of weight they would sound *louder* than this note. A further important factor is that the quaver F does not fall *on* a beat, but on the sub-division of a beat. It must, therefore, be left to the accompanying part to supply the required stress on the second beat.

The accompanying voices do, to a very large extent, prevent the fading of tone in the melodic line. The more movement there is in these voices the greater the resonance they supply to the melody, the sympathetic vibrations set up by them enriching the tonal quality of the whole.

In the following, the pianist will find that it is very difficult to make effective the 'swell' marks when playing the right hand alone. The fading of the dotted minim would appear to call for a cutting away of tone. When the left hand is added the gap is bridged and the fading is not apparent.

Ex. 12. Field

Thus tonal gradation implied in the melodic line often *relies on the accompanying voices* to make it apparent, particularly in slow-moving melodies. This very lovely passage needs sensitive handling of the semiquavers in the left hand and an appreciation of tonal balance:

Ex. 13. Beethoven
Largo e mesto

It is, in fact, very rarely that we find in piano literature a sustained melodic line at a speed slower than andante which is not maintained by a moving accompaniment.

The natural instinct to think music in terms of the voice is

so strong that even reliable editions give us moments of per-
plexity. I have often seen the introductory bars of Mozart's
'Rondeau en Polonaise' from K.284 written thus:

Ex. 14.

The swell on the minim A asks for a crescendo, but how
can this be done on the piano? In actual fact, it cannot, but,
since the music moves fairly quickly, giving the A very little
time to fade, the effect of a tonal build towards the next
strong beat can be got by playing the notes of the third beat
at the *same level* as those of the first, instead of at a lower level
as would normally be correct.

The student who has trained himself to combine instinct
with action, and whose instinct is directed through a sensitivity to sonorities, will not need to go through such an
analytical thinking process, indeed—to quote from Geoffrey
Tankard's book once again—'nuance should not obtrude,
but grow out of spontaneity in music'. This is the eventual
goal, but with many students it is necessary to think and
study on the lines I have suggested before the spontaneity of
the individual becomes one with that of the music.

LEGATO

Though there are many varieties of touch to be considered
in piano-playing, they are all basically of two kinds—
Legato, where the sounds are connected, and Staccato,
where they are not connected. The average pianist is, however, inclined to take it too much for granted that, where he
is not deliberately playing staccato, then he must be playing
legato.

A true legato is attained only by careful listening, and the pianist must listen to the end of the sound, as well as the beginning. Where the music is slow each sound must be given sufficient resonance to tide the gap between the striking of one note and another. In this we have again to take into consideration the fading of the sound. As has already been demonstrated, the sounds within a legato passage should not all be played at the same tonal level: the production of a true legato is dependent on an appreciation of the rhythmic impulse of the music and a corresponding nuance of tone.

The student is more often prone to make a break in the continuity of the sound than he realizes. Certain difficulties which face the beginner do not always appear to have been overcome by those who consider they have passed the early stages of piano-playing. The most common of these is where a legato melody in one hand is accompanied by detached notes in the other. It is better, for the moment, not to take into consideration the result of pedalling such passages—the pedal is not meant as a refuge to cover deficiencies—so I give here two examples of music which does not require pedalling, and in which the joining of sounds in the melodic line depends upon sensitivity of ear and control of fingers in the right hand, whilst the left plays detached notes:

Ex. 15.
Bach

Ex. 16.
Mozart

In this last example it is not uncommon to hear the sections marked ☐ played thus:

Alternatively, the accompaniment may be legato and maintained against a theme containing a variety of staccato and slurs:

It is quite obvious that, in such music, the accompanying part must be completely smooth and controlled throughout: but I have actually heard a performance of this piece in which the left-hand triplet groups were so broken up that the rhythm had become distorted into this:

To cure this fault we tackle the left hand first, asking the student to practise this figure several times before playing a continuous bar of quavers:

From this point the pianist listens carefully and critically when the right hand is added. It is easy for the inexperienced pianist to allow the phrasing of one hand to upset the other, but the *understanding* of the problem is more than half the battle.

Fresh troubles arise when *one hand* plays both legato and a broken line. We do not have to reach an advanced stage before coming across music which demands the ability to do this. Pieces which are graded II or III give us several examples. The following is particularly well known:

To prevent the melodic line from being broken in this way:

attention should be given to the movement of the thumb, which must be lifted in time to strike the next note. The quaver rests below indicate the moment of lifting in actual practise:

The student needs to be able to maintain a legato in at least one part of chord sequences. Exercises such as these will prepare the way:

Even when the pedal is used the legato can be more convincing if made with the fingers. The following passage is truly effective only if the slurs are made with the fingers and practised without the pedal:

¹ See Bach Fugue in B Flat, Book I, Bars 11–18 etc., and Exx. 110 to 110d of this Book.

It is also necessary to be able to change from one finger to another whilst holding a single note:

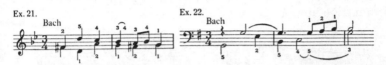

Legatissimo is a superlative of legato and is best described as a very slight overlapping of the sounds: this touch, sometimes known as 'clinging', is occasionally used by experienced artists in slow lyrical passages. It is not wise for the student to experiment too soon with a legatissimo touch unless under guidance, for overlapping of sounds is sometimes a fault caused by the fingers being sluggish in their action. This applies particularly to the fourth and fifth fingers.

The cultivation of a true legato and the cantabile touch which is dependent on it can be attained only if the student has the will to listen and criticize his own efforts and to direct his fingers through a predetermined aim.

REPEATED NOTES

Repeated notes are often badly managed: their frequent introduction into music for beginners leads us to think that this sort of thing is easy:

Once more, the question is not whether it is easy to play the correct notes, but whether it is easy to give each its correct tonal value. It is, for instance, an acknowledged fact that the opening bars of Beethoven's Concerto No. 4 in G can cause the soloist considerably more nervous anxiety than the brilliant runs at the beginning of the Emperor Concerto. The notes, in themselves, cannot be called technically difficult, but the tonal problems are so great that it is said one famous pianist was seen to mop his brow in exhaustion after their execution!

Ex. 24.

In all passages in which repeated notes occur, therefore, tonal gradation must be carefully watched. Even with only two similar notes misaccentuation can disrupt the rhythm. The following extract from a Brahms waltz is an example of this:

Ex. 25.

Notice here the repeated Bs. In each case, were the quaver to be given the same amount of tone as the crotchet it would obtrude into the tonal line causing an apparent distortion of rhythm. Later in the same piece we get this:

Ex. 26.

It is interesting to try playing the right hand alone *without* softening the quavers. Without the steadying beat of the left hand we may get the impression of faulty time values as shown in Ex. 6a. The passage would become in effect:

Ex. 26a.

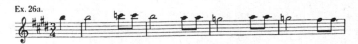

Returning to the field of educational music, one calls to mind many themes from little sonatina movements which can be ruined by monotony of tone on repeated notes. Here are two:

Ex. 27.
Clementi

Ex. 28.
Clementi

In the last example it will be noticed that the repeated notes are marked staccato. This brings me to another point which I feel I must mention in passing. That is the extraordinary tendency on the part of many students to ignore the staccato dot on the last of several repeated notes. Not only beginners are guilty of this fault: I have detected it in performances of music at all grades. A pianist who, in the early stages, plays this little Mozart Minuet:

Ex. 29.

with incorrect phrasing, thus:

Ex. 29a.

will, in a year or two, produce a similar fault in a passage from one of the easier Beethoven Sonatas, so that this:

will become distorted in this way:

If such things are not watched in the early stages, the time will come when the Rondo from the Beethoven C minor Concerto comes in for a similar kind of maltreatment and the theme is presented to us thus:

It would seem obvious that anyone who contemplates playing this work should have overcome such faults, yet this is not always so. Many pianists who have reached what is called a 'concert standard' give us moments of surprise by their apparent unawareness of their own inaccuracies.

Difficulty is frequently experienced when repeated notes appear in legato passages. When *singing* a passage such as the following there need be no break in the continuity of sound, but in performance on the piano (without the use of the sustaining pedal) a break between each D♯ would appear inevitable if the key is completely released before it is struck again:

Here the student will need to experiment, testing the feel and weight of the key, until he can find a way in which legato can be achieved. The first aim will be to make the shortest possible break between the sounds, but patience, coupled with sensitive co-operation between ear and finger, will reveal to the serious student a method of only partly lifting the key, so that he can come very near to a legato in effect.

This sort of problem is more likely to occur in contrapuntal music than any other, and I need hardly add that the same amount of care should be exercised if the repeated notes occur in lower voices:

Ex. 33.
Bach
Andante
etc.

THE SLUR

Tonal shading has also to be considered with relation to the slur. There is no doubt that the interpretation of slur marks cause confusion and misunderstanding. Much experience has to be gained before one can differentiate between the demands of the music and the indiscriminate editing which is to be found in many editions in circulation today. But even where the editing is intelligent and musical there can be varying opinions in the smaller details, and there is no reason why the performer should not form an opinion of his own, *providing* it is after careful thought and study and with a knowledge of the style and period of the composition.

There are certain guiding factors which should help the inexperienced student in his discrimination between logical and illogical editing. The first thing to ask oneself is: Are the slur or phrase marks in keeping with the line of the music? Do they help to make it shapely or do they simply break up the continuity of the phrase? If I were to *sing* the melody would I feel it this way?

A common example of thoughtless editing is where the phrase mark (or slur) embraces one bar at a time without any regard for phrase length, shape, or structure. The two following examples are typical. They have not, for obvious reasons, been taken from any known edition, but I have seen similar phrases equally maltreated:

Ex. 34. Bach

Ex. 35. Chopin

Apart from such markings, which make no sense whatsoever, there is no set standard by which composers and editors indicate phrasing. Some write only the long phrase line, leaving the smaller details and sub-divisions to the performer. Others mark only the sub-divisions, assuming that the whole phrase is understood. Or, where the editing has been very thorough indeed, the complete phrase *and* its sub-divisions are indicated. Sometimes phrase marks are written over passages which are to be played legato and omitted where the notes are detached.

It is indeed difficult for the composer to convey exactly what he intends without confusing the performer. I know from my own limited experience, and with very simple music, that there are moments when I am quite surprised to hear how ineptly I seem to have indicated my ideas!

In explaining some points which may guide the student in his interpretation of the slur I want to make it clear that I am not, for the moment, referring to the long curved lines which show the whole length of the phrase, but to the slur over groups of two or three notes which show the sub-divisions of the phrase. These can be said to indicate a 'manner of performance'.

The most characteristic slurring is that over pairs of notes:

Ex. 36.

When the slur passes from a strong to a weak beat it is usually assumed that the tone fades from the first to the second note, the amount of fading depending on the tempo and mood of the music. With music that is lively and 'busy' the sound fades only a fraction but is completely cut away after the second note of the slur. Typical of this type of slurring is the following passage from a Chopin Waltz:

Ex. 37.   *Tempo giusto*

It will be noticed here that each beat repeats the note of the preceding weaker half-beat. Thus the pianist is *compelled* to treat the slurs correctly (or more or less so!). If, however, this type of repetition is not evident it becomes extremely difficult to play slurred pairs of notes beyond a certain speed.

Ex. 38.   Beethoven
Allegro vivace

In the notes to the Associated Board edition of Beethoven Sonatas the editor, Tovey, says of this movement: 'Limit your tempo severely to that in which you can separate each pair of semiquavers'. A further note warns the student that there may be a tendency to clip them into Scotch snaps (thus).

Where the mood is gay and light the fading sound has the

effect of a short staccato, particularly where staccato notes precede or follow the slurs: *Same as semi-staccato*

Ex. 39. Mozart
Allegretto

The above is typical of music which can have its whole character changed by the observance or non-observance of the slurs. So often are they ignored that modern composers and editors frequently add a staccato dot to ensure the correct performance of the music.

It naturally follows that where the music includes semi-staccato notes the slur ending will take the same degree of shortness:

Ex. 40. Beethoven
Andante

When the music is more sedate, as here, the sound should never be 'clipped', but shaded from the first note to the second.

In the Bach Minuet quoted in Ex. 41 each beat is detached, but only sufficiently to give a gentle lilt to the music as the sound softens on the second quaver. (It will be seen that in bar 3 this effect passes from the right hand to the left.)

Ex. 41. Bach
Allegretto tranquillo

The slower the tempo becomes, the less abruptly the sound terminates. In the following bars the second chord of each pair fades in such a way that one can hardly tell the moment at which the sound ceases. Needless to say, it is not easy to achieve this without constant practice and finely-judged control of key (see also the text dealing with Ex. 185):

When slurred notes are preceded or followed by single unedited notes the phrase will become more shapely if the single notes are matched with the final ones of the slurred groups, i.e.:

The examples so far given have dealt entirely with slurs which indicate divisions of the sound. There is, however, another implication when the slur appears in a flowing melodic

line such as the following. Here a cantabile touch is used and
the slurs seem to suggest a *tonal* inflection rather than a break
in the sound. To cut the phrase into small sections does not
seem compatible with the lyrical vein of the music:

Ex. 46.

The treatment of this and many similar figures becomes a
matter for the taste and judgement of the individual performer and there are bound to be differences of opinion. In
this particular phrase I have heard some performances in
which the slurred beats have been detached and others with
the line unbroken. Both interpretations have been by artists
of unquestionable repute.

The shading of tone is as important in the accompanying
voices as in the solo part. Insufficient thought is given to this,
particularly in the case of phrase endings. Here we can refer
to very simple music and see how clumsy and awkward the
ending will be if the tonal quantity is not carefully matched.
This is one of the lessons which should be learnt in the beginner stages, becoming instinctive in the well-taught pupil.
Here are two typical endings in which the shading of the last
bass note must be observed.

Ex. 47.   Ex. 48.

We now come to the slur which progresses from a weak to
a strong beat. Again we must take into consideration the
tempo and mood of the music and the matching of staccato
or semi-staccato tone. Here, however, there are other factors
which decide whether the accent falls on the strong beat or is
deflected by the slur.

In typical dominant-tonic openings it is obvious that the tonal build is *towards* the tonic:

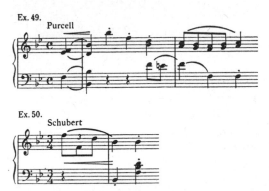

Sometimes the slur sub-divides the phrase after the first beat of the bar, or even after the half-bar. Editions vary, and authenticity is hard to establish, but this type of phrasing appears to be in character.

In the foregoing the break is only very slight, and the first beat must not be abrupt or too soft. It requires to be sufficiently definite in sound to maintain the natural accent of the first beat, for the slur is not intended to indicate a cross-rhythm. I have heard such phrasing interpreted thus, but I feel that it is wrong.

Where the music flows more freely it is questionable whether there should be a break at all. The implication of a slur is rather of a tonal inflection.

With skilful handling an almost infinitesimal break *can* be made at the phrase divisions of the above, but it is better merely to fade the tone and to 'think' the breaks than to produce an abrupt staccato at these places.

The slur from weak to strong beat may, however, imply a displacement of the natural accent:

Here a stress on the first octave A conveys a feeling of excitement and a forward urge to the music. This same forward urge is implied in the development section of the 1st movement of the 'Pathétique' Sonata:

I cannot imagine anyone playing this music without feeling that the accent is diverted from the beat to the half beat.

The slur should also not be mis-interpreted when it is written over the two final notes of a phrase or section, or when a short note value leads to a longer one. In this case the final note (or chord) should be given its full value. The

slur is there to indicate the necessity for a perfect legato.
Here the crotchet * takes its full value:

Ex. 55.

Finally we come to the point where we realize that two
notes within a slur can be of the *same tonal value*. This is usually
where a continuous melodic line is indicated, and yet the
notes of the melody are broken up, by the intervention either
of rests or of accompanying figures. To come to any conclusion about this the pianist must experiment with the melodic
line alone, taking the *whole phrase* into consideration. Naturally we may not all come to the same conclusion, but the
main point is to make the phrase shapely and logical. Typical
is the following:

Ex. 56.

The *visual* appearance of the first slur might lead us to
think that an accent should fall upon the first strong beat,
yet on playing the phrase one feels that the lyrical vein of the
music demands a level tone. It therefore appears that the
happiest solution is to grade the tone as indicated here:

Ex. 56a

In the above quotation the left hand will, of course, play its
own part in the tonal inflection. A brief reference to the

importance of the accompanying voice was made on pages 9 and 10 (see Exx. 12 and 13) and more will be said about the balance between the hands in a later chapter.

The nuance suggested here for the opening bars of this Mozart Sonata is only one of several solutions. The pianist who takes the trouble to study such problems, and who arrives at his own conclusions, is more likely to play with conviction than he who has no predetermined plan. It is the indeterminate performance which must be avoided, for it expresses exactly nothing.

One cannot lay down hard-and-fast rules with regard to the interpretation of every slur, but it is possible to outline a method of approach, and this I have endeavoured to do. If my suggestions and examples prompt the student to give more thought to this aspect of interpretation, then the object of this chapter will have been achieved.

STACCATO

Everyone knows that where a staccato dot is marked the note should be short or detached, but it is not always realized that the degree of shortness varies considerably. Though musical dictionaries have sought to standardize the signs which imply different degrees of staccato, few composers follow their rulings. The student needs to study the music in its context, so that he can determine the interpretation that it demands. Tempo, mood, and style each have to be taken into consideration when choosing the correct type of staccato for a work. I cannot go into great detail here, since, in a book of this kind, it is only possible to give a broad outline. The important point is for the student to realize that staccato can be played in a number of different ways, and to take the trouble to study each work with this in mind.

The most straightforward staccato passages occur in music which has a clearly defined outline, and where the tempo is in general brisk and 'busy'. Two examples follow, out of the

countless ones that come to mind. They require a touch that
is bright and crisp, so that the sounds are clear cut and very
much detached, yet resonant:

Where the music is of a less robust nature, and the touch
is lightened, the staccato might be described as 'pin-prick'.
The works of Mozart abound in themes requiring a precise
and meticulous cleanliness. Such music has been described as
'courtly', 'dainty', 'elegant'—whatever the term the staccato
has this 'pin-prick' accuracy, and much of the resonance is
cut away:

Nor is this touch required only in the works of the Mozart
period. Context and mood should be sufficient to indicate its
use. Certain dance styles, for instance, are usually associated
with it:

In contrast is music in which the shortest possible sound
would be out of keeping with the mood and tempo. In this

we use a mezzo-staccato, which the composer usually indicates by using dots and slur together. (It is also known as portamento, but I prefer the simpler term.) Many passages which are marked as mezzo-staccato might more accurately have been written in shorter note values with rests added, but this procedure would complicate the score. For example, this little piece by Schumann:

Ex. 62.
Langsam

could quite suitably be written thus:

Ex. 62a.

and the staccato in bars three and four of the following:

Ex. 63.
Beethoven
Allegretto

could be written:

Ex. 63a.

Mezzo-staccato is not always indicated by the composer or editor. It is often the performer who has to make the decision.

In this he must realize that short, sharp staccato would destroy the mood of music that is reposeful, sad, or majestic, whereas it would add sparkle to a piece of gay, lively, or humorous character.

It will readily be seen that an over-crisp touch in the following would be out of keeping with the gentle and almost mysterious entry of the theme:

Whereas the opening bars of Schumann's 'Grillen' (Whims) calls for the brightest possible touch.

In music where the mood is lyrical and the movement slow, mezzo-staccato is often combined with legato pedalling. This gives a 'floating' quality to the melody which would not be apparent were the *touch* to be legato:

A combination of mezzo-staccato and pedal is frequently used when there are repeated notes in the melodic line:

Ex. 67.

Schubert
Andante

Ped.————— P————— P————— P

A melody that moves over a strong harmonic bass also calls for the use of the pedal with short staccato groups, particularly, again, where the music is lyrical:

Ex. 68.

Chopin

Ped.————————— Ped.—————————

Such basses as the following, though marked staccato, should be pedalled where they provide a harmonic foundation:

Ex. 69.

Chopin

Ped.———— P————— P————— P—————

In contrast, we get rapid staccato passages in which each note must be clearly articulated. The effect *in sound* at a moderate speed can be produced by playing a scale as rapidly as possible with the third finger: this gives the percussive quality for which we are listening. As the speed becomes quicker, clear articulation depends on the fingers. If the music becomes softer, less energy is used, and the arm adds practically no weight to the hands and fingers. In describing the 'feeling' of playing soft rapid staccato I have suggested to my pupils that they imagine the key depth is reduced, so that the touch has become shallow. Such word pictures seem to help many people to grasp what is required of them better than more technical terms. The following illustrates the type of staccato to which I am referring:

Ex. 70.

When single staccato notes are interpolated into rapid legato passages their implication is not always clearly understood:

Ex. 71.

The above is typical of the many places where the staccato dot implies an *accent*. These notes, therefore, are played with added speed and thrust, causing them to be isolated in sound one from another and giving the effect of a staccato melody. This is highlighted by the crisp staccato of the left hand. A passage of this kind rarely, if ever, does not have a contrapuntal balance to offset the staccato effect.[1]

Sometimes the position of a note within the bar will determine its length. Where the last of two or three staccato notes falls on a strong beat the final note usually takes more

[1] This kind of thinking can sometimes help to determine the phrasing of unedited music, particularly of Bach.

weight and is of longer duration than the others (as at * in the example following):

Ex. 72.

Different lengths of staccato must also be observed if there are notes of different value. In the opening bars of Mozart's Sonata K.284 there should be a difference in length between staccato crotchets and staccato quavers:

Ex. 73.

The ultimate effect of bars 2 and 3 being approximately as follows:

Ex. 73a.

Sometimes we even find staccato minims. A little set of Variations by Beethoven provide an example:

Ex. 74.

One wonders why Beethoven did not write the minims as crotchets with crotchet rests. There certainly must be a difference between them and the crotchets. The whole theme demands a semi-staccato touch and is not as easy to make effective as it appears at first sight.

One could continue to enumerate different sorts of staccato. Indeed, the foregoing only seems to touch the fringe of the subject. I hope, however, that it will set the student thinking, so that he can take the matter up where I have left it.

THE ACCENT

Just as the staccato dot can convey a number of ideas, so the accent or *sf* takes its character from the context of the music.

In the first place it will be obvious that if the passage is 'forte' the accent or *sf*[1] requires greater strength than if it is 'piano'. Compare the following, both from the same Mozart Sonata:

Ex. 75.

Ex. 76

or again, two quotations from a Chopin Waltz:

Ex. 77.

[1] See notes on *sf*, pages 36–37.

Ex. 78.

There must also be a difference in the accent which occurs in staccato passages and that which is implied when the touch is legato. The staccato accent is more percussive, whereas the legato accent has greater depth of tone. In these bars the 'attack' on each staccato accent is sharp and clearly defined:

Ex. 79.
Beethoven

whereas in an earlier passage from the same Sonata the accents need added depth and a penetrating quality, which will add to their sustaining power:

Ex. 80.
Beethoven

Compare also the two examples of accent in the *softer* passages of Mozart and Chopin just quoted (Exx. 76 and 77). The Mozart needs to be 'felt' within the shape of the phrase, whereas the Chopin is 'pointed', to emphasize the light gaiety of the music.

The *sf* or *fz* mark is frequently used in place of the accent. One might surmise that it carries greater depth of tone and would be more likely to appear in music of a more dramatic nature, but comparison of the two signs as used by a variety of composers does not serve to strengthen any particular theory. For this reason I treat the accent and the *sf* as one and the same thing.

Beethoven edited his works very thoroughly where dynamics were concerned, and he employed the *sf* far more than the accent. When the accent does appear, it is usually where a single melodic line is moving quickly and lightly, but even this is not consistent.

It may be that Beethoven's deafness led him to hear, inwardly, a tonal range and variety of which the piano of his day was not capable, and that his striving to indicate his intentions account for inconsistencies of editing.

It appears that we can divide the *effect* made by accented notes into four categories.

1. *The accent which strengthens the harmonic foundation.*

Ex. 81.

The same effect is intended in the *fp*. This is used by Mozart where Beethoven would have given us *sf*:

Ex. 82.

2. *A naturally anticipated accent* which enhances the tonal or rhythmic effect of a figure or phrase, or which stresses the climax (see over).

Ex. 83.

3. *A sudden, sharp emphasis on a single beat* which brings the natural accent into prominence:

Ex. 84.

4. *The unexpected accent,* which (*a*) heightens the dramatic intensity:

Ex. 85.

(*b*) changes the character of a theme, so that this:

Ex. 86.

becomes this:

Ex. 86a.

(c) adds a touch of humour and sparkle:

Ex. 87. Beethoven

(d) serves to heighten the effect where syncopation or cross-rhythms are introduced:

Ex. 88. Beethoven
Allegro molto

Sometimes a series of accented notes will completely displace the normal accent, giving the effect of a change of time. Such a phrase occurs in a gay little Tchaikovsky Waltz from his *Album for the Young*:

Ex. 89. Tchaikovsky

Here, for a few bars, we feel that the music has changed from three to two time. Such effects can be made clearer by the use of the pedal. (See also Section on Cross Rhythm, pages 87–88.)

There are moments when we need to stop and think before deciding just how much tone to give an accented note. We must consider the relationship between that note and others in the phrase. A slight mis-judgement can be unfortunate.

Typical of music which needs this particular kind of judgement is the opening of the third movement of Beethoven's Concerto in B♭. Here one can veer in the direction of 'too much' or 'too little' tone given to the second quaver in each beat of the first bar:

Too much tone, and the effect will become as an anacrusis:

too little, and the point and humour are lost. In this instance I would say that there should be two accented beats: (1) the natural accent (on the first beat) and (2) the accent indicated, which gives the theme its individuality. The first accent has not quite the 'pointedness' of the second, but is offset by the left-hand part, which (for want of a better term) should supply a good 'kick off' to the movement without accenting the second note. Remember, too, that there is an echo of the theme later on, this time in the key of G and with a semi-quaver accompaniment:

This would lose its effectiveness were the *opening* bars to suggest an anacrusis.

Editors, in trying to indicate the nuance of a phrase, sometimes add 'flat' accents over certain notes: ¯ ¯ ¯ These signify added stress to these notes without any sudden sharp accentuation. Such markings can be helpful to the inexperienced student, but they show only one point of view and should not *in all cases* be taken as authentic. It is as well to use music that is not 'over-edited', or at all events is edited by pianists of repute. For this reason I have quoted largely from the works of Beethoven because he edited his own works more thoroughly than many composers.

It is not possible in one short chapter to indicate the innumerable changes of character which can be given to the accent. As always, a study of the context of the music is essential in every case.

THE PAUSE

The most important thing in the interpretation of the pause is its duration in proportion to the music. In a short piece where the music is of a slight nature, a long-drawn-out pause would be out of place, whereas music on a grand scale often demands one that is long and impressive. Apart from this, the length of the pause depends on that which leads up to it and that which is to follow. Frequently a pause is preceded by an allargando, where judgement is required in the grading of tone and speed in proportion to the length of the phrase.

We are all familiar with the grand pause on the dominant chord with which the orchestra heralds the opening bars of a cadenza in the classical concerto. This is almost invariably preceded by a long crescendo—an ever-growing sense of something to come. It is as though the chord says: 'NOW', as the soloist takes the stage. This pause must be sufficiently long to create a feeling of excitement and anticipation.

It has been said that there should be a fractional silence after a pause. It seems to me, however, that there are instances where this does not apply. I have in mind as an example part of the first movement of Beethoven's Sonata

Op. 10 No. 3. Leading to the development section a variation of the opening bars of the movement culminates on a pause which is immediately followed by one of Beethoven's startling key changes:

Ex. 92.

In this instance the pause becomes a 'taking-off place'. It is as though one were poised on a springboard ready to dive, and the moment comes when it is impossible to turn back. There is a forward impulse from the uprushing octaves to the B♭ chord, so that to hold the octave A too long would give the effect of a complete anti-climax. The octave A *leads* to the B♭ chord and I cannot feel that there should be any break in the sound.

By comparison the pause at the end of the development section in the same work plays quite a different role: the excitement of the section has reached its culmination and the sound of the dominant chord must be allowed to fade before the re-entry of the first subject. Here there *should* be that moment of silence after the pause (the comma is mine):

Ex. 93.

The pause sign is sometimes written at the end of a piece of music. It may either be over the final chord or after the sound has finished. When it comes *over* the final chord it prolongs the sound, but where it is over rest or bar line it is there to intimate that the composition is finished and corresponds to the word 'finis' in a book.

A pause written over a bar line anywhere else in the music indicates a momentary silence. In this case the sound preceding it should not be prolonged. Once again the length of silence must be in proportion to the impulse of the music.

Where the word 'ten' (tenuto) is written over a single note it implies a 'leaning' on that note, but the sound is only very slightly lengthened. It is something akin to 'rubato' where a 'lingering' on one or more notes appears to 'stretch out' the melodic line.

I was once told by a little girl that she had always been taught to 'count two extra' for a pause! This certainly seems to simplify things, though I myself cannot agree that musical problems can be solved by mathematical formulae. How easy it would be if they could, but how dull! Once we have passed the stage of learning to play the correct notes and time, music is so personal that there cannot be an exact right and wrong. But there can be good taste and bad taste, good habits and bad habits, and it is to help in the cultivation of good taste and good habits that I am endeavouring to put into words much that is really wordless.

TONAL GRADATION

The most frequently misinterpreted signs of expression are the crescendo and the diminuendo. We teach our pupils that crescendo means *gradually* getting louder, but when the sign appears, what happens? Whether the sound is to be increased from 'piano' to 'forte' or from 'pianissimo' to 'fortissimo', whether the tone is to be built up over a period of four bars or one of eight bars, makes no difference. The student *immediately* jumps to 'forte', and remains at this level until the word 'diminuendo' appears, when, as suddenly, he reduces the tone to 'piano'. It may seem that I exaggerate, and indeed I am speaking only of the worst cases I have heard, but it is a fact that very few pianists give sufficient thought to the exact grading of their crescendos and diminuendos. What must be realized is that the moment at which the sign appears is a starting point. If for instance the music is 'forte' and the word 'diminuendo' appears, the *first note* of the ensuing passage is 'forte' and the sound decreases *from there;* its gradation depending upon the number of bars before the softest tone is indicated.

It has been stated that a pianist can employ at least twenty gradations of tone. This is asking rather much of the average student (and piano!), but everyone should practise taking a single note or chord and, starting as softly as possible, building it gradually to a fortissimo, then once more returning to pianissimo. For such tone building the opening bars of Rachmaninov's Second Piano Concerto provide good practice.

Scales, too, can be practised with all kinds of tonal variety, sometimes increasing or decreasing the tone quickly over one octave, and at others more gradually over four octaves. With younger students I have compared the one octave scale with the ascent and descent of a steep hill, whereas when playing four octaves they are travelling up a gentle slope.

In a long crescendo, care must be taken to see that the 'peak' of tone is not reached too soon, leaving the pianist with nothing further to do at the moment of climax. I have sometimes heard a strange tendency to drop the tone suddenly just *before* the climax of the phrase is reached: this is most unsatisfying to the listener and should never happen unless the composer has indicated some special effect. Similarly, with diminuendo, the lowest level of tone must be correctly anticipated, or the sound will reach the point of 'nothingness'.

There are times when the piano can be compared with the orchestra, in both tone blending and building. We imagine that the mind wields the baton and that the fingers are the instrumentalists. Can anyone imagine a conductor not *listening* to his orchestra? In his hands he holds the capacity for blend and balance, keeping each instrument under his con-

trol, watching and waiting for the moment when the roll on
the timpani brings with it the climax of tone.

But, it will be argued, the piano cannot produce such an
effect as this! Perhaps not exactly, but there are factors which
are comparable, for instance the significance (so often forgotten) of the left hand in the building of tone. I often tell my
pupils to keep something back in the left hand as a 'reserve of
power' for the final climax.

The Sonatas of Beethoven call for continuous judgement
in these matters. This scale passage from Op. 10 No. 3 can be
fully effective only if the amount of weight behind each note
is controlled by the mind of the pianist:

Ex. 94.

Again, in the last movement of the same Sonata a rapid
rise and fall of tone calls for some quick thinking and responsive fingers:

Ex. 95.

Returning to the first movement we see that the final crescendo covers nine bars of broken chords, commencing thus:

Ex. 96.

Here the increase of tone is passed from chord to chord rather
than from note to note, the intervening quavers carrying the
ear forward to the next harmonic change. Tone building in
such a passage should be practised as a series of block harmonies:

Ex. 97.

It is always helpful to reduce a broken chord passage to
block harmony, especially where the pianist is undecided as
to the nuance and shape of the whole. Indeed, it is also a
good practice if younger students have difficulty in learning
or memorizing the actual notes. Their hands are then *shaped
over the chord* instead of over one note at a time, and the playing becomes more fluent. I have found that pupils who at first
imagine the Bach Prelude in C, Book 1, to be little more than
a study, will appreciate its beauty *and* learn it more quickly,
if they first play it in this way:

Ex. 98.

Such examples make it clear that the crescendo does not
pass from note to note, but from beat to beat. An apt illustration is found in Sidney Harrison's *Beginning to Play the Piano*

(O.U.P.). Here he asks the pupil to repeat the words 'Louder and *louder* and LOUDER'. In this way the pupil is made to realize that the loudest syllable was not the last. In fact, a phrase containing pairs of slurred notes following a crescendo should sound something like this:

Ex. 99.

The same applies, in reverse as it were, to a phrase from Beethoven's 'Pathétique' Sonata; here the tone is built from half beat to half beat (the implied accents caused by the slur marks indicate this):

Ex. 100.

This idea leads us a step further, to the appreciation of tonal nuance within a crescendo or diminuendo. The phrase that follows is built on a sequential pattern, each figure having its own shape *within* the crescendo:

Ex. 101.
Beethoven

The building of tone, therefore, is from 'peak to peak', and the nearest that can be indicated in writing is this:

Ex. 101a.

(Notice also that the left hand enters on the *softest* note of each figure.)

The grading of a long diminuendo seems to present less

difficulty—the approximate grading, where there are pairs of notes should be:

Ex. 102.

At all times, therefore, the pianist must think ahead. There is a strange paradox here, for, though he must listen to every sound as he makes it, he is also anticipating that which is to come. It has been said: 'In rehearsal look back, in performance look forward'.[1] Thus the 'listening' in rehearsal is immediately critical and, in performance, anticipatory.

Finally it must be understood that no tonal gradation on the piano is successful unless the quality of each register of the individual instrument has been studied. Many instruments have very thin tone in the higher octaves, and on such instruments tone that is consciously decreased towards the treble may fade too much. On the other hand, there are many pianos with a very resonant bass, and on these the effect of a crescendo towards the lower register could become thick and muddy if not sensitively controlled by ear and fingers. Thus an understanding of the problems and possibilities of each individual instrument is essential if the student is, eventually, to become a polished performer.

TONAL BALANCE
MELODY AND ACCOMPANIMENT—CONTRAPUNTAL MUSIC

A large amount of piano literature contains pieces which are, in themselves, melody with accompaniment. Music for beginners, especially of the Classic and Romantic periods, abounds in this. Many composers who have written supposedly easy pieces have set the young pianist other prob-

[1] Attributed to Sir Adrian Boult.

lems besides the correct performance of notes and time. Typical is this little piece by Schumann:

Ex. 103.
Schumann

I very much doubt whether one in a hundred of the young pianists who are learning this piece today make it sound as Schumann 'thought' it—a song in the right hand with an *accompaniment* in the left.

I have always felt that, in the early stages, insufficient stress is laid on the importance of controlling the balance between the hands—possibly some teachers may feel that they are lucky if they get the right notes at all, and that there isn't time for this sort of thing. In any case it would be quite beyond the pupil. But would it? I have found that the average child will take up any challenge and that there is more fascination in trying to make a specified sound than in simply pushing down the right key. Though this book is not primarily about beginners, it is in the early stages that this tonal balance should be acquired. Here is a very simple exercise for those who have difficulty in varying the touch between the hands. Let them play a one octave scale in the centre of the piano *very slowly*, the left hand to start on C and the right hand on the E a tenth above. First the right hand is played 'forte' and the left hand 'piano', then the process is reversed and the left hand plays louder. This exercise is simple, but there are pianists in all grades who would do well to practise it.

It will, by now, have become apparent that this book is more concerned with 'what we want to do' than with 'how to do it', and much can be done by having an *intense desire* to produce the required effect; however, where tonal balance is concerned, it is helpful to demonstrate that 'arm weight allied to firm finger tips' produces a warm singing tone, whereas a light arm and less finger exertion helps to soften the tone. The two contrasted movements can even be practised on a table! In the end it is the desire *behind* the physical conditions that enables the pianist to control his tone.

This does not mean that all melodies from now on are to be played 'forte' with 'piano' accompaniment: the exercise is only a preliminary to the control of various permutations of tone. It was recently said to a competitor in a music festival: 'Your melody does not sing, you should soften the accompaniment.' What sound advice this was, and how much better than the reverse process in which the melody tries to outshine whatever noise may be going on. It reminds me of the conversation of a number of children where each tries to be heard above the other until the result is complete bedlam! Thus the student, once he is able to 'bring out the melody', should not push it mercilessly at the audience with no regard for the mood and tonal level of the music, or for the importance of its harmonic foundation. Even if the bass is purely accompaniment the foundation notes must be given sufficient depth to prevent the music from becoming top-heavy.

A typical bass of the eighteenth century, known as the Alberti bass, was widely used by many of the sonatina writers of that time. Millions of young pianists must have churned their way through Clementi, Kuhlau, Diabelli, and others with little thought for the actual effect they were producing. A feature of this bass is the constant reiteration of tonic-dominant broken chords, and the dominant note, usually played with the thumb, is repeated endlessly. It is the insistence of this note which gives the churning effect to which I have just referred. To overcome this defect the student may be told to soften the left hand, but such advice is not quite correct, for the *basic* notes of the harmonies are important and must be heard. It is the *thumb* which must be softened, together with any other notes that play only a subsidiary part in filling in the harmonies.

Many delightful little sonatina movements deserve more thoughtful treatment than is given to them. Characteristic is this well-known movement from a Clementi Sonatina:

Ex. 104.

In this opening phrase there is no harmonic change and little interest appears to be given to the left hand, yet the left hand can do much to add life and rhythm to the melody. To begin with, there must be a firm entry on the first D, followed by a cutting away of the tone on the three quavers that follow. These three quavers, being constantly repeated, need watching, but they can help in the build-up of tone in the second half of the bar, because they act as a counterpoint to the rising quavers in the right hand. The right-hand climax, A, is given added resonance by a good strong accompanying bass note after which the left-hand quaver tone must once more be cut back.

The second subject of the same Sonatina provides a charming contrast, but here again we are faced with the problem of the left thumb: seven bars of repeated Es (twenty-eight Es in all!). No wonder the music can sound monotonous if not sensitively treated. Here are the first few bars:

Ex. 105.

There is no doubt here that the left-hand thumb must be softened *throughout* the section, the lower notes in the accompanying part supplying the resonance to the melody. I spoke

in *The Young Pianist* of what I called the 'skeleton structure',
and it always appears to me that, if music of this type is reduced to a bare outline, the student is more easily able to
assess the tonal nuance of the accompanying voices. Here,
then, is an outline of the structure of Ex. 105:

Ex. 105a.

It will be seen that such basses are not intended to be
meaningless and flimsy and that tonal balance depends on
the sensitivity of their handling. Where accompanying parts
provide a melodic line which is contrapuntal to the theme the
two voices should be balanced as in a vocal duet. This
balance is required in the two following quotations from the
little Beethoven Sonata in G Op 49 No. 2:

Ex. 106.

Ex. 107.

In each case the left thumb is softened, and the duets
emerge as:

Ex. 106a.

Ex. 107a.

A familiar type of accompaniment, in which the left hand plays repeated chords on the weaker beats over a changing bass, comes in for a good deal of thoughtless treatment. This is sometimes called an 'Um-cha-cha' bass, but from the way many people play it I think the term 'Um-plonk-plonk' might be more suitable! The Waltzes and Mazurkas of Chopin suffer particularly in this respect, the heaviness of the chords causing the life and sparkle to be lost from some of the loveliest of his melodies. These chords must of course be lightened, whilst the lower bass notes maintain a firm rhythmic precision.

There seems to be a tendency to play any old thing where these lower notes are concerned, and the number of bad shots is often out of all proportion to the difficulty of the music. It is not always appreciated that wrong notes and uncontrolled tone can be the result of incorrect fingering. Many students use the little finger far too much in these accompaniments, taking it continuously from lower note to chord and back again. Ease of arm movement brings with it increased accuracy and lightness, but this cannot be achieved when the fingering is ill chosen. It will be found that if the lower bass notes are taken with the fifth finger and the lower notes of the chords with the third or fourth finger, there will be a lateral swing of the arm which ensures greater accuracy and ease.

This will illustrate my point:

Ex. 108.

Bad fingering

Ex. 108a.

Sometimes of course it may be necessary to use the fifth finger on a chord where the stretch demands it, but it should be avoided whenever other fingering can be managed.

The second fault, which also makes the accompaniment more difficult to play, is very similar. This is where wrong fingering is chosen for pairs of chords having notes in common (one is usually an inversion of the other). Here the fingering should be arranged so that the notes in common are taken by the same fingers. If the two chords are practised *as one* the correct fingering will be determined.

Ex. 109.   Bad

Ex. 109a.   (The chords as a whole)

Ex. 109b.   Good

I stress the importance of fingering in these examples so that the student may learn to play such accompaniments with ease, instead of making heavy weather of them and detracting from the flow of the melody.

Has my treatment of this subject been too exhaustive and tedious? Have my remarks on the Alberti bass and chordal accompaniments been too obvious? I fear that many of my readers may think so. But I write only of what I hear, and I must insist that, at the present time, I hear only a very small proportion of aspiring pianists conveying an understanding of these simple principles *in their performances*. It is of no use to know a thing unless we can communicate that knowledge to others. Once again I beg for a greater measure of self-criticism from those who are studying to become pianists.

I should like to go a little further with this problem of balance between the hands, still considering music which is a definite song with accompaniment. What to do with the song is often fairly obvious, but the art of accompaniment is a study in itself, whether we are accompanying singers, instrumentalists, or ourselves. All pianists should make a point of getting the experience of playing with other people. Ensemble music is an enriching and rewarding pastime for the pianist, who tends to become very self-centred in his music making. The 'give and take' between one instrument and another develops a sensitivity of ear and broadens the outlook. Not only this, it will increase the understanding with which the pianist accompanies himself. There is a tendency among inexperienced accompanists to imagine that they should keep entirely in the background. They do not seem to realize that the foundations of the music as a whole lie in their hands, and that the mood of a song is often conveyed by the harmonic structure and the movement of the piano part. Neither is it only in the more technically difficult music that the accompanist has problems. Gerald Moore says, in his delightful book *The Unashamed Accompanist*: [1]

'I maintain that to play such a song as "The Erl King" does not require nearly so much thought as the playing of Schubert's "Litany" and "Du bist die Ruh" (Thou art peace to me). In these songs each note has to be played with due regard to the note that preceded it and the note that succeeds it and be properly proportioned in the whole musical sentence.'

The 'arranger' who takes well-known piano music and re-edits it for piano and violin is not very popular with the

[1] Ascherberg, Hopwood, and Crew.

serious musician, yet I sometimes feel that I should like to buy his copies (providing they were in the right key and that all the notes were there!) and present them to some of my pupils. This might save me endless trouble in trying to explain a method which I have found invaluable in the teaching and playing of melody and accompaniment.

Let us suppose that the student is learning the first of the Schumann *Kinderscenen*:

Ex. 110.

In this piece the melodic line is written over a flowing accompaniment, and it is of greatest importance that no note of the accompaniment should obtrude. It is quite common, however, to hear a performance which gives this impression of the melody:

Ex. 110a.

A suggested practice method for a piece of this type is as follows:

First play the melody alone, legato (students who are working without guidance are reminded that in this piece the melody is contained in the notes which have the upper stems in the printed copy):

Ex. 110b.

This should be played and memorized. The accompaniment is then 'separated' from the melodic line, thus:

Ex. 110c.

The student will now see, by referring to the original text, that the right hand maintains in its upper part a cantabile melody, and in its lower part the third quaver of each accompanying triplet. The next stage, then, is to balance these sounds in the *right hand alone*, making the upper voice sing and playing the thumb softly. Care must be taken to see that the upper voice is still played legato:

Ex. 110d.   etc. throughout

This preliminary practice should be done without using the sustaining pedal, though it will need to be included in eventual performance. (The student would do well to refer to Exx. 173 and 173a when pedalling this piece.)

Now we come to the second section.

Ex. 111.

Here a counter-melody is introduced in the bass, and the lower notes should be practised in the same way as the melody in Exx. 110b and 110d. This section of the piece has a richer texture and can be thought of as a three-part song. It could, in fact, be played as such before the accompaniment is added:

Ex. 111a.

This scheme of practice need not apply only to a melodic line and its accompaniment. We find accompanying parts in which the hand is similarly divided. Examples can be found in the bass of the Brahms Waltz in E (Ex. 26) or in the first eight bars of the Chopin Waltz (see Ex. 179).

If the accompaniment includes repeated notes care must be taken that none are left out. I have often had to correct pupils of mine who have brought this version of the Minuet from a Beethoven Sonata:

Ex. 112.

in place of:

Ex. 112a.

Frequently, one hears, too, part of a Chopin Prelude:

Ex. 113.

played in this way:

Ex. 113a.

It is a case, here, not only of hearing the correct texture, but of *feeling* the repeated notes under the fingers, and many students who cannot always detect such faults by listening should be able to correct them by the feel of the notes. I do not wish in any way to minimize the importance of listening continually, but this particular fault is an insidious one, and all students may not have sufficiently keen ears to detect it, especially when listening to the playing of another part. The desire to bring out the melody may cause the whole concentration to be centred on it, resulting in missed notes in the accompaniment. (Refer also to p. 14.)

It is a case not only of grasping these things ourselves, but of making them clear to the listener. We think we are doing so because we hear the sounds we expect, but expectation is not always the same as realization, and it is through our fingers that we convey the significance of the musical structure. If we listen to a recording of our own playing we may be surprised by unexpected faults of tonal balance and rhythmic variety. Tape recorders provide a wonderful means of opening our ears to these faults, and the owners of such instruments can make good and intelligent use of them. But it is not a good thing to use them *continually* during practice. True self-criticism needs no medium, for the reaction to sound should be immediate. The ability to listen critically to our own playing is essential, and if we always rely upon a later play-back the edge may be taken from our own aural perception.

In connection with the Schumann piece referred to on pp. 56–57, I drew the reader's attention to the three-part song in the second section. Such contrapuntal devices are often not made clear if the student concentrates on one line of the music to the exclusion of all other voices. This certainly means that he has acquired some ability to balance the tone, but this ability must be used with intelligence and with due regard to the structure of the music. A work which often receives the wrong treatment is the Schumann Romance in F♯, simply because, in their enthusiasm to bring out this lovely melody, many pianists do not observe that it is not a solo but a *duet*, around which the accompaniment is woven:

Ex. 114.

This is frequently played with a lovely singing tone in the lower voice of the *right* hand and a complete failure to realize the importance of the upper notes of the *left* hand, which are in fact the partner in the duet:

Ex. 114a.

This particular work provides wonderful opportunities for varieties of tonal balance, the duet moving after the double bar to the two upper voices of the right hand.

Ex. 115.

Five bars later the interest again moves, this time to the two outside voices, which play in canon towards the climax of the section. Frequently, however, the importance of the bass part is not appreciated, and the canonic device is not made clear by its manner of performance:

Ex. 116.

It is largely a matter of visual perception, for when the semiquaver accompaniment is omitted the canon becomes clear to the eye:

Ex. 116a.

This visual perception could be called the 'hearing eye'! It is certainly essential that the teacher of advanced pupils should develop this faculty. It is always possible that the student may bring a work with which the teacher is not familiar, and no lesson can be called satisfactory unless he or she can quickly and completely grasp the structure of the music and give constructive criticism that will help the pupil.

Such quickness of eye is invaluable to the sight-reader, who needs a keen perception to observe where the melodic interest passes from one hand to another. I well remember, as a child, setting out during my school holidays to learn the second movement from the Beethoven Op. 14 No. 2. I managed to grasp the fact that this music was in theme-and-variation form, but when it came to *playing* the first variation I could not at first understand where some of the melody had got to! What a thrill it was when I finally discovered the 'missing notes' which had (all unobserved by me at first) slipped away from my left to my right hand!

To quote the whole section would be rather a lengthy business, but my readers will, I feel sure, recognize the work if I quote from it the two phrases which, at first, eluded me.

Ex. 117.

Ex. 118.

The music of Brahms, in particular, gives us repeated instances of the melodic line weaving its way in and out of
other parts. From many suitable quotations I have chosen
here one from the Intermezzo in A, Op. 118 (Exx. 156–7 also
illustrate this):

Ex. 119.

In this music we also notice figures which are echoes or
fragments of earlier themes, such devices being characteristic
of Brahms, in whose works no single note ever appears to be
redundant. Echo themes such as these are not always observed by the pianist, and many sink into obscurity so that
their significance is lost. One that often seems to pass unnoticed comes from Debussy's 'Clair de lune':

Ex. 120.

Tonal control becomes more and more important as the student advances through the grades. The ability to make one or other note come into prominence is largely attained through the will to do it. Where a melody lies at the top of chordal music there must be a singing fourth or fifth finger, the highest note being struck with more key speed and firmer finger than the others. This gives a typical example:

Ex. 121.

Schubert

I have heard many performances of this piece in which equal weight is given to all three notes of the right-hand chords. The result can only be called 'stodgy' because the melody has no life of its own. To overcome this the student should first practise with the right-hand part divided between the hands, realizing, as he does so, that the upper voice is the song and the lower chords the accompaniment:

Ex. 121a.

Having listened carefully to this effect, he endeavours to produce the same tonal balance whilst playing the right-hand music in its original form. If the result is not what he hoped for, exercises are improvised on the lines of the simple one suggested on page 49. This time, however, two notes are taken in *one* hand—a series of sixths will do to start with—and the student tries to bring out the higher or the lower at will. Eventually this should be possible with three or even four notes, but such control may take months or years of hard and determined effort. Ability to do this becomes essential in the performance of more difficult contrapuntal music. The pianist who wishes to play the fugues of Bach should make sure, first, that he can give clarity to his part playing in two-part works. In these not only must each part be clearly outlined, but it must have individual life and tonal nuance.

It is a misconception to think that all Bach's music is purely contrapuntal. We have only to look at the delightful little pieces in the Anna Magdalena collection, or at many of the shorter dance movements in the Suites and Partitas, to appreciate that here are singable tunes written in the form of melody and accompaniment. The accompanying voices, however, are also full of interest, and are an integral part of the whole. It is on the shapeliness given to them in performance that the effect of the music will often depend. The following is a good illustration:

Ex. 122.

In many of Bach's works the melodic line flows as a series of lovely phrases which, though they form part of the structure of the whole, are never 'worn out through constant repetition'. The listener who likes a 'good tune to hum' does not always take readily to these long melodic lines because he cannot fit them into his limited conception of 'a tune'. The sensitive performer, however, by his own appreciation of their line and nuance, can do much to entice the ear and point out the shapeliness of the melody. A wonderful example of such melodic fertility comes near the beginning of the F minor Clavier Concerto. This movement is often played too quickly and the lovely line of melody tossed off with little regard for the significance of each phrase:

Ex. 123.

One such melody that *has* achieved popularity is the Air from the Suite in D for Orchestra (erroneously spoken of as 'Air on the G string'). In this the charm of the melodic line is still further enhanced by the interweaving of other voices. Bach's keyboard music, too, gives us many moments when the interweaving of voices demand, from the pianist, a sensitivity to the relationship between one part and another.

There are many instances in the music of Bach that lead us to believe that he thought of music as pure sound, independent from any one particular instrument. Now that the whole of keyboard literature has devolved on the piano, and only a small minority of performers play it on any other keyboard instrument, there is a tendency to treat works of completely different texture with a monotonous sameness. We should appreciate, for instance, that, where music built on broken chord figures would have been effective on the harpsichord, with its small bright tone:

Ex. 124.

music built on sustained chords would be admirably suited to
the clavichord which was capable of sustaining the sound:

Ex. 125.

It will sometimes be found that a flowing melodic line
alternates with broken chord figures giving a key to the correct tonal balance of the phrase through its harmonic structure. Thus the tonal line of the following:

Ex. 126.

is clearly seen by a study of the harmonic structure:

Ex. 126a.

In such passages, then, the weight should be slightly released
on the notes marked *.

Ex. 126b.

It is essential to release the weight where one voice is subservient to another, or else the dominating melodic line will
be confused with other voices, so that clarity suffers. In the
next example my *fp* (not marked in the printed copy) in-

dicates where the tone should be cut away, leaving the crotchet to sing over the alto voice.

Ex. 127.

One frequently hears a performance of this phrase which gives the following impression:

Ex. 127a.

I have discussed in some detail problems which arise in the performance of Bach, because the student who realizes these things has the key to the performance of all piano music. Of course it is not only in music of the contrapuntal period that thought must be given to part playing: the few examples that follow will show how alert the pianist needs to be to tonal balance in music of all styles and periods. In each case I have given first the full context, then the melodic line as it should be, then the melody as it is *often* heard.

Ex. 128. Beethoven

Ex. 128a.

Ex. 128b.

There are of course occasions when one hand is given two voices, which appear to be of equal importance yet must each be heard as a distinct and separate line. I have often told my pupils that were such music to be written for the orchestra, and the two parts taken by, let us say, an oboe and a flute, both players could play at an absolute level of sound and the two voices would be clearly divided, because of the difference in *tonal* quality between the two instruments. On the piano, however, with a tonal quality that is (or should be) the same throughout the instrument, it is very difficult indeed to separate *in sound* two parts which are played *at the same level of tone*. Experienced artists do, by a subtle manipulation of tonal nuance, create the illusion that this can be done, but for the average performer another way may have to be found.

If therefore two voices are of equal importance, the only way to give them clarity of line is by varying the tonal *quantity*, that is, by playing one a little louder than the other. As an illustration I have chosen a passage from a Haydn Sonata:

Ex. 131.

It is usually found that the division is made clearer if the higher voice is brought into prominence, but this must, of course, depend on the context of the music. In this case we will divide the parts in such a way that the top voice is *mf* and the lower voice *mp*, and take one part in each hand, so that we can hear the effect of this:

Ex. 131a.

Once the ear is accustomed to this tonal balance, the same effect is achieved, through practice, in the right hand alone. Here there will be a fingering problem and finger changes (as indicated) will enable the student to maintain a better legato:

Ex. 131b.

Many students give insufficient thought to the preparation of such passages. I have often heard the phrase here quoted played in a manner which conveyed the wrong idea to the listener:

Ex. 131c.

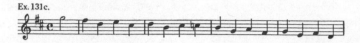

In all such things lie the difference between the good and the bad in piano-playing. Right notes may be commendable up to a point, but without tonal colour they are like inanimate objects. Music must live, and the pianist brings mere notes to life by the thought that lies behind his fingers. There should therefore be an intelligent and thoughtful approach to each piece of music that is studied. I spoke in the Foreword to this book of a 'listening desire', which means, of course, that the pianist must have some kind of an idea as to what he intends to do. We have travelled a long way in this chapter, but I hope the many examples given may help the student to formulate his own ideas with regard to the interpretation of the music he is studying.

TEMPO AND RHYTHMIC VARIATION

A suitable choice of tempo is of utmost importance in the performance of any work. Though the musician is primarily guided by the composer's indications, such as 'adagio', 'andante', 'presto', etc., there is a latitude within the limits of such indications. There cannot be an exact right and wrong, and the tempo chosen must be one that suits the temperament and the technique of the performer.

On the whole there is a tendency to play fast music too fast and slow music too slowly. It should be realized that in a lively piece the effect of speed and brilliance can be more easily felt if there is clear articulation than if the sounds are flimsy and indefinite. For this reason the pianist who adopts a slower tempo may give more sparkle and glitter to a piece than one who rushes through at a speed beyond his control.

In the case of slow music it takes a great artist to maintain the continuity and to sustain slow-moving sounds so that they do not completely fade, thereby halting the impulse of the music. I have discussed the fading sound earlier in the book, and pointed out that the more slowly the music moves the more skilfully will the sounds have to be matched. I once listened to a record of Beethoven's 'Moonlight' Sonata in which the pianist, a very great artist, takes the first movement as slowly as it has ever been played. In spite of the beauty of this performance I would not advise the student who listens to such a recording to try to imitate it. There is a danger in too much studied imitation. Enthusiastic listeners who try to make an exact copy of what they hear are not only stifling any personal interpretative sense they may have, but are playing by imitation instead of by inner conviction. Undoubtedly we can learn much that will influence our performance but, in the end, the music has to speak through *us* and *our* fingers! The performance of a great artist is an inspiration and guide but not an inflexible copy.

This applies also to the teacher, who may guide, advise, and correct, but who should never impose rigid ideas on his or her pupils to the extent that they all play one piece in exactly the same way. Spontaneity is essential in the development of interpretation, and where music is learnt in a parrot-like fashion it is lost, and with it a feeling of conviction.

At the opposite ends of the tempo indications are the terms 'presto' and 'largo'. These leave little doubt as to their meaning, and what I have just said about very fast or very slow playing may guide the student within the limits of their range. It is, however, in the intermediate speeds that misunderstandings sometimes arise. The term 'allegro', for instance, denotes that the music shall be lively and the touch bright, but the speed at which a single note-value is taken varies considerably. A comparison between, not only the works of varying composers, but also the works of one composer, will bear this out.

These two movements from Beethoven Sonatas, both marked 'allegro' and both in 3/4 time, could not possibly have the same speed for a dotted minim:

Ex. 132.

Ex. 133.

The addition of the words 'con brio' denotes an increase of vigour and attack and does not directly refer to speed, but where 'con brio' follows the term 'allegro' the natural tendency is to obtain the increased vigour by livening up the speed.

It must be realized that the tempo indication refers to the speed of a *beat*, not of its sub-divisions. Particularly significant is the difference between C (four crotchets in a bar) and ¢ or Alla breve time (two minims in a bar). Where the mark is ¢, the speed of the *minim* beat can be equal to that of a *crotchet* in 2/4 or 4/4 time, as these two opening phrases will show:

Ex. 134.

Beethoven
Allegro (M.M. = ♩ 104 approx.)

Ex. 135.

Realization of the *beat* is particularly important in music marked 'andante'. This means 'moving along' at a leisurely walking speed, but such movements as the following are often played so slowly that to walk to the *crotchet* beats would mean adopting a funereal gait.

Ex. 136.

If the tempo indication is andante (or quicker), it is essential that music in *compound time* should receive its proper impulse. Early in his training the student should have learnt that 6/8 means two beats in a bar, 9/8 three beats, 12/8 four beats, and so on. The pianist who 'thinks' compound time according to the *sub-divisions* of the beats is almost bound to adopt too slow a tempo. If, for example, a piece in 9/8 time is thought of as having nine beats in a bar the music will certainly move too slowly. I have heard performances of the following in which the graceful flow of the music was replaced by a stagnant sentimentality:

Ex. 137.

As I have said earlier, suitable speeds for lyrical melodies can usually be determined if they are *sung*. The phrase endings correspond to breathing places and the melody flows continuously from phrase to phrase.

Once the tempo has been decided upon, *it must be established from the very first beat*, unless, as in exceptional cases such as the following, the composer has indicated a pause on an anacrusis:

Normally the anacrusis must be felt within the basic pulse of the whole. Frequently one hears this sort of thing:

It is also quite common for the pianist to start a piece of music at a quicker tempo than he can manage in the more difficult sections, so that after a time a noticeable slowing of the speed is heard. This is more easily detected by the teacher or critic than by the performer, and those who are studying alone would be wise to check speeds on a metronome, however rock-like they may believe their basic pulse to be. Different rhythmic figures can play strange tricks with one's aural perception, and the pianist who is quite convinced he is neither hurrying nor slowing the tempo may have a surprise if he resorts to such a check.

I have frequently heard my pupils cheerfully romp through the first subject of Beethoven's Op. 2 No. 2 at an approximate metronome speed of ♩ = 132

Ex.140.

only to arrive at this:

Ex. 141.

where the speed drops to about 112! Having listened to several lines at this new speed (and by now the student has comfortably settled down to it) I set the metronome ticking in time with the playing. 'Now', I say, 'let's go back to the beginning.' Needless to say the pupil is quite amazed at the difference in the speed. The same applies to hurrying, though this is more difficult to control if due to nervous excitement. Slow technical practice in which the beats or half beats are accented will help to give a feeling of stability, and a knowledge that the fingers are safe should reassure the performer in times of stress. The chief thing is to *know* which sections we are liable to hurry; we can then exert a conscious 'pulling back' at these places.

Really bad deviation from the basic pulse is the most unforgivable of all faults. It must undoubtedly be the strongest reason for failing a candidate in any examination, and no other merits in the performance can adequately counteract it. Some years ago a lady came to me for piano lessons, informing me that she had already entered her name for a Diploma examination in two months' time. She brought me the Beethoven Sonata Op. 10 No. 1 (a frequent Diploma choice) and we started off with the first movement. It is no exaggeration to say that she played no two sections of this movement at the same tempo; she must have adopted at least six different speeds, varying from M.M. $\downarrow = 132$ to M.M. $\downarrow = 192$.

The lady was utterly shocked when I produced a metronome with which to compare her varieties of tempo, and informed me that such a device was completely out of date, and allowed no artistic licence whatsoever. Needless to say I lost the pupil, for which I was greatly relieved! But I must hasten to say that I do not expect anyone to play *to* a metronome throughout any piece of music, except for practice of sections where the fingerwork is uneven or the time hurried. However, for setting, checking, and comparing speeds it is invaluable and should be looked upon as a necessity by all serious students.

Now we come to the 'artistic licence' about which my lady-friend was so anxious. What exactly is it? It has been described as rhythmic freedom—elasticity—give and take, and indeed any of these terms will do, providing the interpretation of the word 'licence' is always qualified by the word 'artistic' and that the performer's idea of artistry is within the bounds of good taste.

The musical term applied to this rhythmic freedom is 'rubato'. Around this term endless controversy has raged, and on its interpretation the greatest of pianists and teachers have had opposing views. Stop-watches have been used to prove that a phrase played twice, once with and once without rubato, should take the same number of seconds. It was found, however, that an exact rule could not be applied, for, as Percy Scholes puts it in *The Oxford Companion to Music*, 'an artistic principle may exist as a principle, and offer valuable guidance to the student, without there being any great possibility that it will ever be carried out by human beings with exactness'.

It can be said, however, that rubato is a flexibility of time *within the phrase* and that it should not appreciably change its time scheme. At one time rubato was described as a freedom *within the measure or pulse*, but it has been realized that to attempt time variation and correction in so short a unit can only result in rhythmic distortion.

When I was a child I used to watch the swing-boats in the annual fair which visited our town. As the boat swung higher and higher, so it paused a fraction of a second at the peak of its climb, only to swing back with increased speed as the pause lengthened. Since then I have often thought how aptly this illustrates the principle of rubato.

An essential to properly balanced rubato is that the performer should have a good sense of rhythm. The pianist who cannot maintain a steady and unflagging rhythm in a Bach Prelude is unlikely to produce an artistically balanced rubato in a Chopin Nocturne. Rhythm and rubato are interdependent, and not diametrically opposed.

The music of Chopin, demanding as it does a frequent use of rubato, comes in for more rhythmic abuse than that of any other composer. In the past, pianists, good, bad, and indifferent, adopted what has been called a 'personal' style in playing Chopin. Fortunately this vogue is out, and sincerity has largely taken the place of personal display. Where individuality is evident it is the result of a conviction within the performer, and few pianists adopt a style so individual that the music itself becomes subservient to the (so-called) artist.

There is, however, a difference between this 'personal' style which I have decried and the fact that certain soloists and conductors appear to have an unusual affinity with the minds of specific composers. This affinity is usually the result of intensive thought and study, and is apparent only where the interpreter seeks to identify his thought with that behind the work to be performed. It is not just a case of 'I like it this way' or 'I feel it this way'; there must also be a knowledge of period and of the style of the composer. Above all, there must be artistic integrity.

This digression may appear to have little bearing on the meaning of rubato. But I used the words 'artistic licence', and wished to stress the fact that there are two opposites in this respect—artistic abuse and artistic integrity—and the first has, at times, been paraded under the guise of individuality.

It is thought by many people that rubato should not be introduced into any work that was written before the Beethoven period. There is, however, evidence that composers who lived before this time, Mozart in particular, had other views on this. I myself feel that a very discreet elasticity may be allowed in music of a lyrical nature. I have in mind some of the slower movements by Bach and Mozart.

Some may ask: 'Is there all that difference, then, between "tempo rubato" and "ritardando", in view of the fact the latter is bound to be followed by "a tempo"?' Indeed there is a world of difference. For though both imply a checking of the basic pulse, the former does so *within the phrase* and does not necessarily culminate in a point of rest, whereas the latter usually leads to a phrase end or stopping place. Rubato is also more instinctive, relying on personal feeling, whereas a ritardando is placed in a definite position by the composer.

The ritardando itself (and similarly the rallentando) must be properly proportioned to the speed of the music. It is a common failing to check the rhythmic impulse too abruptly. Where 'poco a poco' is added over a number of bars the music will reach the end of its impulse long before the end if the slowing-down process is sudden and exaggerated. The music should come to rest as smoothly as a well-driven motor car arrives at a pre-determined stopping place. An effect akin to 'emergency breaking' can be just as uncomfortable for the sensitive listener as for the unwary passenger in the car! There is a similarity between this and the sudden dropping of tone in a diminuendo to which I referred on page 44.

In the case of 'meno mosso' there must be an *immediate* change to a slower tempo, which, having been established, continues until altered by a further tempo indication. This, then, has only a distant relationship with the ritardando. It will follow that the same difference is felt between 'accelerando' and 'pui mosso'.

If the words 'senza rit.' appear they should be faithfully observed, for obviously a composer will only mark a 'senza rit.' if he desires just that special effect.

There are instances where the illusion of a slowing tempo is created by the lengthening of note values as the music draws to a close. This very effective device should not be exaggerated by a deliberately added 'rit.'. The last few bars of Brahms's Rhapsody in G minor give a clear illustration:

Ex. 142.

The words 'l'istesso tempo' are not always clearly understood. Indicating that the performer should maintain the same speed as before, they often occur where the unit of the basic pulse is changed. For example, if the time changes from 6/8 to 2/4 the new crotchet beat is taken at the same speed as the previous dotted crotchet beat. In other cases (particularly when the music is in the form of variations) 'l'istesso tempo' is used where the actual figuration itself is changed and yet the basic tempo is to remain the same.

The pulse of music is sometimes said to be its 'life-blood'; occasional wrong notes, or even deliberate misreadings (though regrettable), are far less likely to detract from a performance than ill-chosen tempi, wrongly judged rhythmic variations, or unexpected vagaries in the speed.

TIME PROBLEMS

As the pulse in music may be called its life-blood, so variation of rhythmic figure determines the mood, character, and individuality of the whole.

A familiar tune, played in an unaccustomed time and rhythm, can become almost unrecognizable:

Ex. 143.

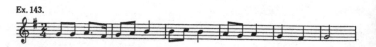

When the time remains the same as the original and only the note values are altered the tune becomes recognizable, though few people would fail to notice such discrepancies as in the following:

Ex. 144.

It is, however, in inaccuracies of the smaller sub-divisions of the beat that lack of rhythmic integrity is so often apparent. Time is the arithmetic of music, and if we learn our arithmetic properly we shall understand the time values which sometimes cause difficulty.

Dotted notes come first in this category. They should be part of the early training, but it is not uncommon to hear dotted notes wrongly spaced by players who have passed the beginner stage. A correct response to a dotted note is comparable with the correct answer to an arithmetical problem. No one would pass G.C.E. maths. if he were 'somewhere near' the correct answers, yet students expect to pass music examinations with rhythmic figures that are nowhere near the correct time.

I once asked a new pupil to explain a dotted crotchet: her answer was: 'A kind of a jerky note.' From this I gathered that her musical arithmetic had not reached the stage of fractions! The sub-division of the beat is entirely a matter of fractions, and were the dotted crotchet always thought of as $1\frac{1}{2}$ beats exactly (a crotchet plus a quaver) it could not possibly be played out of time. Those who have only thought of it as a 'jerky note' should play it against an even flow of quavers. Such a procedure cannot fail to bring it into line. When, for example, this little piece is learnt:

the practice method will be:

or, as an interesting alternative:

Either of these methods should cure any tendency to 'double-dot' the dotted crotchets.

With dotted quavers there is a strong inclination to subdivide the beat into three instead of four, so that this rhythm

 could be played only against a flow of triplets, which is of course incorrect. The practice method should be similar to that for the dotted crotchet.

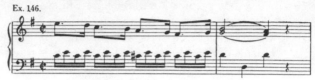

Ex. 146.

An inversion of this rhythm often causes trouble. In the performance of such passages as the following:

Ex. 147.
Mozart

we usually get:

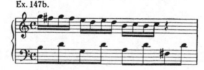

Ex. 147a.

To instil accuracy of timing it could be tried like this:

Ex. 147b.

Then, when the speed of the semiquaver has been firmly established, the extra notes are omitted.

There are, of course, instances when variation from the strict dotted value *is* permissible, but here knowledge of style and period is needed. It is a fact that, before the time of Mozart, the dot was freer in its timing. This is lucidly explained in the following quotation from Percy Scholes's *Oxford Companion to Music*:

'In older music (up to and including Bach and Handel) the addition to the note was approximately half, and the exact rendering was left to a combination of tradition, taste and common sense. Thus in:

the rendering would usually be:

and in a very slow movement ♩. ♪ would be rendered ♩.. ♪ ... To meet this last case Leopold Mozart, in the year 1769, introduced the use of the double dot. . . .'

A typical example of this rhythmic combination

can be found in Bach's Prelude in D, Book II, bars 5 and 6.

It is not uncommon for the dotted crotchet and dotted quaver to appear within the same bar or phrase. In such a case exact rhythm must be observed. Consider the third phrase of the Clementi Sonatina quoted in Ex. 145:

Ex. 148.

In this case the tendency will be to 'double-dot' the crotchets marked *, so that the following quavers become semiquavers. Thus a uniform speed is given to quavers and semiquavers which is *not correct*.

The triplet presents a new problem, because here the beats are sub-divided into three—not a natural process in simple time. The instinct is to retain the natural sub-division and present the triplet thus: ♫♩ To realize the equal spacing of the sounds the student should think forward to the next strong beat, the three triplet quavers flowing evenly towards it, thus:

The tendency to stop after the third quaver may also be overcome by fitting words to the figure. I have often successfully taught my younger pupils to play the triplet in a little Bach Minuet to these words:

Ex. 149.

o - ver the moon   we   go.

If the triplet is correctly felt when it is first encountered, there is a reasonable chance that in later years the student will not give us this version (not uncommon) of a Chopin Waltz:

Ex. 150.[1]

The use of words for the realization of rhythmic figures will always be found helpful. Any jargon will do providing it fits the rhythm! There is a cult, however, in which beginners learn the rhythms of *all* their pieces by repeating rhymes and jingles. Such a method will defeat its own ends if word patterns consistently replace a knowledge of time values as interpreted from the printed page. All pianists must be able to associate the visual with the aural, and too much simplification of the basic elements will result in complications at a later stage.

When a continuous flow of duplet quavers is immediately followed by triplets there will be a tendency to lose the speed of the pulse and to slow down the music.

Ex. 151.

Beethoven

[1] A correct version is found on p. 103.

The student must realize that notes of the triplets are going to move faster than those of the duplets, and a little practice with the metronome will help him to appreciate this. As a preliminary to the correct timing of the triplets a short section could be selected for special practice:

Ex. 151a.

L.H. alone here

In compound time, however, it must be realized that triplets are a *natural* subdivision of the beat, and it is the *duplet* which requires care with regard to its spacing. The appearance of the duplet in compound time is not very common, but where it does occur the beat (now a dotted note) must be divided into two *equal* halves.

Ex. 152.   Debussy

(For realization of the duplet quavers against semiquavers see bar 41 of the above piece 'Clair de Lune').

The *visual* grouping of notes into threes does not always denote that the *accentuation* falls on the first of each group. Sometimes the grouping merely indicates the division between the hands, where the melodic line passes from one to another.

The Prelude in D♭ by Glière is typical:

Ex. 153.

This is frequently played with an accent on the first of each group of three notes, giving the effect of 12/8 instead of 6/4. Though both these times have the same number of quavers, the sub-division of a half bar (or dotted minim) differs. In 12/8 it is ♩. ♩. and in 6/4 ♩♩♩ Thus it will be seen that accentuation in quaver triplets causes a 'cross rhythm'. To cure this misaccentuation, the piece should be practised with a conscious accent on each crotchet beat:

Ex. 153a.

A pupil of mine once brought the same type of rhythmic misreading in the first movement of the Schumann Concerto. (I write the accentuation as she made it):

Ex. 154.

This, in effect, is as though the section were written in 12/8 instead of 6/4, and though she stuck to it manfully, we had several bars of unexpected cross rhythm which Schumann never intended!

Ex. 155.

Such a misunderstanding might cause complete disintegration had the accompaniment been with an orchestra instead of on a second piano. (I feel that I should add she gave a successful performance with orchestra later!)

Where cross rhythms occur the problem is more a matter of 'proportionate accentuation' than of arithmetic. The accentuation of the varying parts depends on their relationship with one another and with the new rhythmic impulse. If the cross rhythm is felt equally in all parts the effect will be of a temporary change of time. The Tchaikovsky Waltz quoted in Ex. 89 gives a clear example of music in which a change from 3/4 to 2/4 time is momentarily implied.

Brahms frequently used such rhythmic devices, and his compositions may be said to provide more examples of cross rhythm, cross accentuation or cross time than those of any other composer. Typical is the Intermezzo in C from the Op. 119, in which the original theme is augmented so that the 6/8 time becomes for the moment 3/4:

Ex. 156.

Ex. 156a.

If, as in the above, the cross rhythm appears in the melodic outline whilst the accompanying figure maintains the original pulse, the effect is of a cross accentuation. This I have implied by grouping the quavers according to the pulse. Though these beats are not deliberately accented they must continue to be *felt* in the left hand.

If, on the other hand, the cross rhythm appears in the *accompanying* parts, the natural accent is not noticeably displaced, yet the cross beats have a life of their own which is sustained by the awareness of the performer:

Ex. 157.

One could give endless examples of interesting changes effected by such rhythmic devices. One of the most fascinating comes from the third movement of Schumann's Piano Concerto. This is a form of augmentation that appears to double the length of a beat, so that music which is written in 3/4 time gives the impression that it has changed to 3/2. In this example I give the melodic line only and, below it, the rhythmic impression conveyed to the listener:

Ex. 158.

Yet, throughout the performance of such a section, the *feeling* of the 3/4 pulse must never be lost by the performers.

Cross time, most commonly known as 'two against three' or 'three against four', is, once again, a matter of arithmetic. I gave a detailed lesson on this in *The Young Pianist*, and here I will only give examples of each of the above with a key to its arithmetical proportions. My example of 'two against three' is taken from a Haydn Sonata, the smaller notes denoting the common rhythm made by the two parts:

Ex. 159.

A well-known example of 'three against four' (the cause of many a headache in the teaching profession) is taken from the Field Nocturne in B♭:

Ex. 160.

The 'common rhythm' as a separate unit is more easily realized in notes of longer value. Thus this: is an exact representation of the rhythm in Ex. 160.

Slow practice may be necessary before the student can play cross time with natural ease. Simple exercises can be evolved, built on five-finger groups. (See those in Book IV of *At the Keyboard*.)[1] The speed of these is gradually increased, and then the relevant passages are practised in the same way. But to practise such rhythmic figures isolated from the complete piece will not ensure that they can readily be made to fit in to the whole. The sudden advent of a cross-time passage may have a paralysing effect on the student, causing him to lose the regular pulse of the music and to adopt a completely different tempo for the cross-time section. Though

[1] Joan Last. (O.U.P.)

this section is played with conscientious care and correctness *as a separate unit*, the speed of the *pulse* may be completely different from that which has gone before. When, however, the passage is completed, the student will probably return to the original tempo.

This means, then, that the first consideration must be given to the speed of a *beat*. For example, when 'two against three' occurs in simple time the speed of a *triplet* is established in exactly the same way as outlined on page 84, Ex. 151. The 'two' is then fitted into the 'three', *not* the 'three' into the 'two'.

Let us take an example from Mozart K.332:

Ex. 161.

It will be found useful to practise this in stages, thus:

Ex. 161a.
1st stage of practice

Ex. 161b.
2nd stage

Finally the duplet quavers are restored.

The same method applies to the practising of 'three against four' passages. In the one quoted from a Field Nocturne (Ex. 160) I often find that my pupils play the quaver quadruplets much too slowly. This breaks up the rhythmic flow,

and, however correctly the 'three against four' has been
learnt, there is a halt in the forward impulse of the music.
To overcome this I have found the following practice method
helpful (the accents indicate the four beats, which the pupil
should count out loud in the earliest stages of practice):

Ex. 162.

It may take some days or even weeks of practice before the
passage is played with ease. Eventually some 'give' in the
rhythm is desirable, but strict tempo should be adopted
during the initial practising, until correct timing has been
achieved with certainty.

When the initial beat of a cross-time figure contains either
a rest or a tied note, it is better to replace it by a definite
sound in the first stage of practice. Thus the left hand of these
two bars of Grieg's Nocturne:

Ex. 163.

becomes in practice:

Ex. 163a.

This establishes a steady quaver beat against which the
duplets can be played and from which to hear the 'common

rhythm' made by the two parts. Finally, when the rhythm has been safely established, the ties are restored.

Eventually the pianist reaches a stage where conscious arithmetical calculation ceases to be necessary, indeed until this stage is reached there can be no real continuity of thought behind a performance. Such calculation is hardly advisable in passages in which the hands have unequal groups of notes whose relative speed is almost impossible (and certainly not practical) to determine in terms of fractions. In such passages each part has an independent life and flows freely towards the next appointed 'meeting place'.

A detailed survey of the so-called 'time problems' in musical notation reveals the fact that, where difficulty is experienced, it is almost invariably due to lack of basic knowledge and understanding. Where the arithmetic is made clear the difficulties melt before our eyes. It is only because far too many students have learnt these things in a haphazard way that I have thought fit to go into the matter in some detail.

PEDALLING

With such an overwhelming emphasis on the function of the fingers, it is not always remembered that much piano music cannot be successfully attempted without an understanding of the use of the pedals, particularly of the sustaining pedal.[1]

This pedal has been described as the soul of the piano, and on its use or misuse the success or failure of a performance may depend. Frank Merrick tells us that 'the sympathetic vibration consequent on lifting the dampers from the strings, imparts a "glow" to the tone'.[2] The word 'glow' is most expressive, and I cannot think of a term that would be more suitable.

With the development of the pianoforte, and because of the new sustaining power it possessed, the style of keyboard writing underwent a gradual change. The works of Mozart

[1] Or damper pedal.   [2] *Practising the Piano* (Rockcliffe).

and Haydn show a need for the use of the pedal in a discreet way, neither is it beyond the bounds of good taste to use the pedal in the contrapuntal music which was written before the advent of the piano: for surely there must be a case for using the mechanism of the instrument to the best advantage, where for instance it effects a more sustained legato, or prevents the tone in lyrical passages from becoming too dry. But since the clarity of the parts in such music must never be blurred, too little pedal—or none at all—is preferable to too much.

Beethoven may be said to be the first composer who exploited the possibilities of the sustaining pedal to the full, and to play his music without it is unthinkable. The romantic period brought forth a wealth of piano literature for which the sustaining pedal is necessary. Yet students often fail to realize that the technique of pedalling needs to be as well understood as that of the arms, hands, and fingers. Preliminary exercises should therefore be practised, to enable the student to know what he is doing with the pedal *before* it is introduced into any piece of music.

The ability to pedal becomes essential in legato passages in which the sounds cannot be completely joined by the fingers. Though the effect of pedalling can be much more far-reaching than this, it must be the first consideration. An amusing description came to me from an enthusiastic amateur, who told me that, to him, the function of the pedal was 'to hold on to one note whilst he was hunting for the next'! Actually, he was not far wrong, and *because he used the pedal objectively*, he never failed to change it correctly.

Correct pedal changes are determined by a communication between ear and foot in the same way that correct sounds are produced by a communication between ear and finger. In both cases *the ear is the guiding factor*. Two or three years ago a student brought me the slow movement of Beethoven's 'Pathétique' Sonata. The lesson had to be given in a town in which I was lecturing, and we were not able to find a very good piano. The upright at our disposal had a short, high pedal, which needed to be depressed with great determination before the dampers responded. After my pupil had played the first section I intervened, suggesting that the music could be made more effective with the use of the sustaining pedal. 'But,' she replied, 'I *am* pedalling!' Her ear had not told her that she had never once moved the dampers from the strings!

It must be understood that it takes longer to dampen the sounds of the low notes than of the high ones: this is due to the added resonance of the longer, thicker bass strings, which need more than just a fleeting touch to stop their vibrations. The very highest strings—usually about $1\frac{1}{2}$ octaves—have no dampers at all, for, being short and thin, they have very little resonance and their sound dies naturally. A question frequently asked is how the pedal can add sustaining power to these high notes, as indeed it does. Here we must remember that, in depressing the pedal, we are lifting the dampers from *all* the strings, and though we may only be *playing* the higher notes a sympathetic vibration is set up throughout the instrument.

This vibration can be demonstrated in a number of ways. The first realization of its significance came to me when, as a member of a school orchestra, I sat with my fingers resting on the strings of my cello whilst the A was given. My instrument must already have been in tune with the piano, for I felt the A string vibrate under my touch. The same effect can be got with two pianos, if one pianist plays a passage whilst the other depresses the pedal without touching the keys. When the first pianist has finished playing and the second continues to hold the pedal down, the strings of his instrument will be heard to vibrate for some considerable time. An even simpler method is to put the mouth close to the strings and sing or yell! If this is done with the foot off the pedal nothing will happen, but if the dampers are first lifted the result will be quite startling. A longer, louder 'echo' is pro-

duced with a grand piano, but the result with an upright is
quite adequate for demonstration.

Owners of upright pianos are reminded that these will give
more resonance when standing across the corner of the room
than when flat against the wall. The advantage of the grand
is that the soundboard, being horizontal, is in line with the
floor, but not *against* the floor. When the perpendicular
soundboard of an upright lies close to the wall the sound
waves are partly deadened immediately they leave the
instrument.

We see, then, that the pedal is a very sensitive mechanism,
and as such it requires sensitive handling.

When the student first learns to pedal he gets the 'feel' of
the 'down–up' movement, maintaining contact with the pedal
with the sole of his foot, and keeping his heel firmly anchored
to the floor. I mention this here because many advanced
students treat the pedal far too violently, making a noisy
tapping with the foot or causing the instrument to give forth
an angry roar! Alternatively there are many whose changes are
not clean because they have not accurately gauged the height
and depth of the pedal. Since this differs on all instruments, it
is advisable to test each one for 'feel' beforehand—particularly
before a public performance, examination, or competition.

Directly the student begins to use the pedal he will realize
that, in playing a series of legato chords, the 'down–up' is replaced by a 'up–down'; here *the moment at which the pedal
is taken up* is more important than that at which it is put
down. When playing such chords as the following, it is *released* at the exact moment when the new sound is made: it
is then depressed again.

Ex. 164.

Schumann

Ped.____ ____ ____   etc.

The time lapse between these two actions must depend on the depth of notes to be dampened and the speed of the music: the ear can be the only guide in this.

With accompaniments such as the following the lower bass notes must be 'caught' by the pedal. This needs fine co-operation between foot and hand, the finger clinging to the lower note until the dampers have again been lifted; it may seem to be a fraction longer than comfort allows, and separate practice of the left hand will be necessary before the fingers can travel unerringly to the chords that follow. Basses of this kind are often played in a 'slap-dash' manner, ruining the effect of the melodic line (see also pp. 53–54):

Ex. 165.

bass from Chopin Waltz.

A slower foot action is necessary where sustained chords are played on the lower register of the piano. In the following bars the dampers must be allowed to remain on the strings sufficiently long to stop the vibrations of the lower bass notes. This means a longer wait after the 'up' movement:

Ex. 166.

Chopin

Those who listen sensitively will notice that the *absence* of pedal at the psychological moment can be almost as detrimental to the effect as over-pedalling. Thus, in this passage from Beethoven, the sudden 'bareness' of tone caused by lifting the pedal on the final minim chord—and not depressing it again—takes all the 'glow' from the music and leaves us cold and disappointed!

Ex. 167.

For similar reasons it will often be found that to add the pedal to a series of unisons will enhance the tone quality in music of a lyrical nature. Pedalling, as indicated below the un-accompanied notes in the following passage, will prevent a sudden feeling of 'bleakness' in music which has previously consisted of sustained harmonies:

Ex. 168.   Chopin
Sostenuto

The addition of the pedal will also enrich the tone of de-tached unisons or chords requiring a big tone, by increasing their sonority. Here, however, the foot moves up and down *with* the hands, allowing the dampers to remain sufficiently long on the strings to maintain the detached effect. This is called 'staccato pedalling' (or 'direct pedalling'). In the ex-ample that follows I give alternative pedalling in the first two bars, the third bar having the *strongest* case for staccato pedal-ling:

Ex. 169.
Schubert

It is extremely difficult to *start* pedalling a legato phrase on any other beat than the first. In true legato the weight is

transferred from the bottom of one key to the bottom of the next, and in this process there must be an infinitesimal moment of overlap of two tonalities. This is not heard so long as the dampers return to the keys at their appointed time, but if the pedal is put down *during* this 'overlapping moment' it can cause an unwanted dissonance. For this reason, in passages similar to the one here quoted the pedal marked *
must be put down *late*, that is, just after the new sound has been made:

Ex. 170.

* pedal down just after the G is struck

Sometimes the merest touch of pedal is needed so that a figure, or phrase, may be in character. The Bach Prelude from which these opening bars are quoted is both serene and expressive, yet the repeated chords in each figure tend to break the melodic line and change the mood, unless very skilfully handled. A touch of pedal, as indicated, may provide a solution:

Ex. 171

Again, many pianists need to cover up the difficulties of a small stretch. Indeed, the average hand cannot cope with all the phrases in which a legato is indicated. The fleeting use of pedal offers a solution in such moments as the following:

Ex. 172
Beethoven
Allegro

The introduction of pedal into broken chord passages must
be coupled with sensitive control of the *fingers*. In the following excerpt the notes marked * are shaded off *before* the
pedal change is made. They only have to be held a fraction
too long to be caught in the new harmony and heard
throughout its duration.

Non-observance of details by the fingers can, indeed, cause
a very unmusical 'blurring' of harmonies.
This:

has often been made to sound like this:

which is most unpleasant to the ear!

Having learnt to change the pedal correctly in chord progressions, some people seem to develop a horror of allowing
any apparently inharmonious note sound to blend with the
basic harmony. It must be realized, however, that isolated
notes or chords are made effective only by their relationship

with others, and that an endless series of concords, however beautifully played, conveys no contrast of emotion. The
playing of a single major chord leaves us unmoved, but if it is
preceded by its dominant seventh we experience both anticipation and realization. Without discord music would become unbearable—something like living on a daily diet of
sugar cakes and sweetened water!

So we must consider the question of pedalling over dis-
cords, or, as I would prefer to put it, over passing notes. This
seems to cause little trouble when crotchet beats are pedalled
during a continuous flow of quavers, but when the 'dotted
quaver-semiquaver' figure appears the foot begins to waver.
Consider the following:

The pedal release marked at * in the above example is *wrong*.
It causes the semiquaver chord to be caught in the C major
harmony that follows, continuing as dissonance for the
duration of the new bar. The correct place for the 'up' pedal
is the moment at which the C major chord speaks, the
'down' following immediately after the sound has been
made. Thus the moment of dissonance is fractional and only
serve to impart an 'edge' to the sonority of the whole.

The pedalling of scale passages might on first thoughts
seem inadvisable, but on examining the possibility we find
that our decision must be influenced by several guiding
factors. These are:

    1. The presence or absence of harmonic foundation.
    2. The speed of the passage.

3. The compass of the notes.
4. The volume of tone indicated.
5. The direction in which the passage is travelling.

These conditions are not placed in any particular order, for they are interdependent one upon another. It will be found that at least two of them will be present in any passage that is selected.

Let the reader first experiment with a short run from the Chopin D♭ Waltz:

Ex. 176.

Play this passage in the following ways (on each attempt the pedal must be depressed):

1. *Without the Left Hand.* (*a*) Slowly and loudly. (*b*) Softly and quickly. (*c*) Softly, an octave higher. (*d*) Softly, two octaves higher. (*e*) Softly or loudly, an octave lower.

2. *With both Hands.* Using the same formulae as above.

It must be realized that many other permutations can be thought out, but by now my readers will have formed very definite ideas on this subject without any further preamble from me. The only condition not yet considered is the direction in which the scale travels, so let us take two more examples, the first from the Chopin Nocturne in F♯ minor, the second from the Brahms B minor Rhapsody:

Ex. 177a

Ex. 177b

Both runs are usually pedalled: in the first the pedal from low C♯ adds to the impression of 'mistiness'—enhancing the effectiveness of the diminuendo (marked in this case 'smorzando')—in the second it adds to the brilliance and helps to build a crescendo which would not be possible were the resonance of the lower notes to be lost. There is some difference of opinion as to whether in Ex. 177b the pedal should be held down from the low G♭ or added after the first octave—conflicting directions come from editors of repute. It appears to me that this cannot be decided until all exterior conditions have been taken into consideration—the resonance of the instrument, the technique of the soloist, and, above all, the acoustics of the room (see also pages 112, 113). Having agreed then that, all things being equal, pedal can be added to ascending scale passages, let us try the last passage in reverse, at the same time depressing the pedal. It will immediately be apparent that the effect is most unpleasant, the sounds becoming so blurred and 'thundery' that all musical and harmonic sense is lost.

Having come to a decision about the conditions which determine the pedalling of scale passages, it will be seen that many cadenza-like runs, trills, turns, arabesques, and the like can be made more effective when the dampers are lifted from the strings throughout their execution, and the choice of pedalling is determined by their harmonic foundation rather than by their own melodic line. This is constantly borne out in the performance of music by Chopin, and it would be superfluous to single out any example from the hundreds

which come to mind. It must always be remembered, however, that such pedalling should only be considered when the
period and context allow.

When the melodic line moves slowly the process is reversed, the
pedalling being directed by the melody rather than its harmonic foundation. Here, for example, the dampers are returned to the strings after each quaver, the chords being sustained with the fingers:

Ex. 178.
Beethoven
Largo e mesto

It is in the 'borderline' cases that personal choice is most
evident, and, in these, pedalling can vary according to pre-
vailing conditions. Where the melody moves at a moderate
speed, for example, I have seen in many editions of Chopin
Waltzes pedal indications which do not appeal to me at all.
These indications are in accordance with the harmonic structure, but I myself prefer to be influenced also by the melody.
Thus we get in some editions the pedalling marked as at (*a*)
and in others (to which I also adhere) as at (*b*):

Ex. 179.

Now let us consider the relationship between pedalling and
phrasing. It may perhaps seem late in the chapter to introduce this important aspect of pedal control, for some might
say it should have been the first consideration. In this I feel
like the hostess who, having invited a number of distinguished

guests to dinner, is in a fever of anxiety as to how they should be seated! For it is quite impossible to assemble all the facts influencing the choice of pedalling and place them in order of importance. I felt, however, that I could make my points clearer by discussing the unit before the whole.

The phrase length determines the breathing places, and if the breaths are disregarded we get an unbroken line of sound from beginning to end of a piece of music. This gives an effect which can be quite exhausting to listen to, for again we feel the need of contrast, this time the contrast of sounds and silences. The dampers must therefore be allowed to remain a fraction longer on the strings at certain significant phrase endings, and at the culmination of sentences. The audience is thus able to 'come up for breath'. The exact placing of these silences and their length can only be determined by the individual, for it is obvious that no two artists will bring an identical interpretation of any one work. But a knowledge of phrasing and form, and a study of the rhythmic structure, should guide the pianist in his decisions.

Carelessness or ignorance with regard to phrase endings may easily be betrayed by pedal changes. This is particularly evident when the phrase begins or ends on a beat other than the first. The following extract from a Mozart Sonata gives a very clear illustration, for each phrase continues on the same harmony as the previous ending, tempting the unwary to pedal over the phrase changes instead of clarifying them by returning the dampers to the strings (as marked):

Ex. 180.

A similar example is this, in which the pedal is sometimes erroneously held down for the duration of the first bar and changed on the C major chord.

Though it can be said that, as a general rule, phrase endings indicate a pedal change, the pianist must never sink into an easy complaisance in such things, for there must be exceptions to every rule, and the advent of such complications as cross rhythms, overlapping phrases, or cross harmonies may cause him to think again.

With experience the artist learns to use the pedal *for effect* so that the details of staccato, slurs, and phrasing can be given more point by the use of complementary pedal changes. In such details the pedal may be said to 'cross the t and dot the i'. Quite an easy piece which gives opportunities for interesting pedal effects is the fifth of Grieg's *Poetic Tone Pictures*. I will quote three short sections, with suggested pedalling. Bars 1–4:

Bars 19 and 20:

Ex. 183.

Bars 39–43:

Ex. 184.

The moment and manner in which the pedal is lifted have a definite bearing on the effect. In bars 1 to 4 of the last example it was lifted sharply. In the one that follows, as also in the chords in Ex. 42, it is lifted gently and a little late:

Ex.185.
Chopin
Andante sostenuto

Many editions of Chopin Waltzes and Mazurkas give monotonous 'one-in-a-bar' pedalling. Let the student use a little imagination and see what he can do to convey the gaiety and character of the music. Here is just one suggestion, from a very well-known piece:

Ex. 186.
Vivace

It will now have been appreciated that the art of pedalling includes a knowledge of knowing when *not* to pedal, and that the moment and manner of lifting the pedal is as significant as that of depressing it.

It is not a fault to pedal over rests. There is no hard-and-fast rule, though it has been said that the pedal should be lifted for the duration of a rest in music which was written before the time of Beethoven. But whilst such a rule must hold in music of the contrapuntal school, there will surely be exceptions in the case of some works of a lyrical nature which were written during the Mozartian period. I have in mind slow movements such as the following (Ex. 187). In this I have marked the pedal to be held down throughout the fourth beat, allowing the fading melody to merge into the basic harmony. It seems to me that to lift the pedal at this point would impart a dryness to the music which is out of keeping with its song-like character:

Ex. 187.

Here is another instance. The melodic line 'floats' over a broken-chord accompaniment, and a complete break in its continuity would surely add a dryness which is not desirable in this movement:

Ex. 188.

This is analogous with pedalling over staccato notes (Exx. 66–67), and the guiding factors are the same.

In giving these examples from Mozart it may be said that I am voicing an opinion, and that others, more qualified to speak than I, would disagree with me. It appears to me, however, that where the first essential of any piece of music is its lyrical beauty pedalling should be added for effect, rather than deleted for propriety.

On reaching the romantic period the outlook becomes different. The rest, which in contrapuntal music represents a silence, now often becomes a 'tiding-over' period, and where it follows the lower bass harmony this tiding over is a sound, not a silence. Here follow two excerpts, in which the effect of raising the pedal after the initial low note is struck could be compared with that of pulling the foundations from under a house after starting to build it:

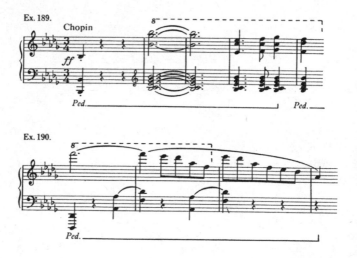

Ex. 189.

Ex. 190.

The impressionistic composers often denote the length of pedal by the value of the lower bass notes:

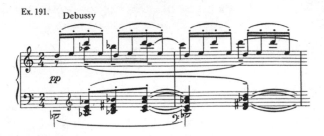

Ex. 191.   Debussy

These composers taught us to listen for new harmonies and unusual blendings of sound. The pedalling of their music may be said to be in exact opposition to that of the Mozartian period. Thus a piece by Mozart would be ruined by too much use of pedal, whereas one by Debussy depends for its effect on the continuous skilful use of the damper mechanism. It seems that we are dealing with two contrasting qualities in these periods, *sound* and *effect*. The classical writers thought of their music in terms of pure sound, whereas the impressionistic writers considered it in terms of effect. This does not mean that their works bear no clearly defined harmonic scheme but, rather, that they introduced a new blending of sonorities whose effect depends very greatly upon an understanding of pedalling and half-pedalling (see page 110).

Nor must it be forgotten that from these writers we get occasional works of a more percussive nature. For example, in the well-known 'Golliwogg's Cake-Walk' we are back at the place where effectiveness of staccato and slur depend on the moment and manner with which the pedal is *taken up*.

Contemporary music, also, will be found to have a far clearer harmonic scheme than the sceptics allow. It is not so much a question of whether harmonic progressions are evident at all, but of whether we appreciate the harmonies used. The student who has studied the art of pedalling in relationship to music of the classic and romantic periods should have little difficulty in determining his pedal changes. When the writing is purely percussive the pedal is reserved for special dynamic effects, but this cannot be said to apply only to the present era; it applies to all music of a percussive nature.

'Half pedalling' must now be mentioned, and I would like to try to clear up a misunderstanding with regard to this term. The appellation is descriptive of the *effect* rather than the *cause*, the aim being to get rid of some of the sounds, whilst others are retained. To do this the dampers must be returned to the strings for a fleeting second—so quickly that the lower vibrations have not had time to lose their resonance. The action, then, is a 'quick pedal', and the result of the quick pedal is that the higher sounds are damped, whilst the lower ones remain. It will be obvious that this can only be done when the lower sonorities are to be preserved. Thus the term 'half pedal' does not imply that the pedal must be only half lifted or half depressed—the movement remains a complete one. It is in regulating the *speed* of pedalling that judgement is required, particularly as all pianos have a different weight and depth to their pedal mechanism.

Half pedalling could well be used in passages such as the following:

Ex. 192.   Debussy

A form of half pedalling, in which several quick 'flutters' of the foot may be necessary, is sometimes called 'tremolo pedalling'. This is done to hasten a diminuendo when the sound built up has become too resonant to allow a softening of the touch to take effect:

Ex. 193.

Because the term 'half pedal' has been applied to an action
that is in fact a 'quick pedal', it is natural for further confusion to arise in the mind of the student over the difference
between this and 'half damping'. Here the pedal *is* only half
(or partly) depressed, causing the dampers to release their
full grip of the strings, yet to remain closer than they would
if the pedal were used normally. In the words of Victor
Booth, this 'gives a gentle buzz to the sounds'.[1] Though this
method of pedalling is effectively used in contrapuntal music
it is not recommended except to the very advanced and experienced pianist. I include it here because questions on this
type of pedalling so often confuse students who enter for
their diploma examinations.

Some pianos, notably the Steinway and the American
Baldwin, have a third pedal. This is in the middle and has
been called the sostenuto pedal. It is attached to a mechanism which catches any dampers that are *up* at the *exact*
moment it is depressed and which remain up until it is
released. Thus the performer is able to sustain *one particular
note or chord*, whilst other sections of the music pass through
unrelated harmonies. It is a pity this mechanism is not
widely adopted as it enables the pianist to follow the wishes
of the composer in no uncertain way.

Finally we come to the soft pedal, one that is often left
severely alone by both teachers and pianists. Why is this?
The most lovely effects can be produced by its use. On a
grand piano the depression of this pedal causes the keyboard

[1] *We Piano Teachers* (Skeffington).

and hammers to be moved sideways, so that two instead of three strings are struck. The most usual action on an upright is for the hammers to be moved closer to the strings, so that they are travelling with less speed at the moment of impact. Taking the grand piano as the ideal it will be noticed that the new position of the hammers causes them to strike a less worn, and therefore softer, portion of the felt. The result (on a piano that does all it should) is an individual tone, sometimes described as atmospheric. The soft pedal should not therefore be used whenever the word 'pianissimo' appears in the score, but rather should be reserved for moments when the special tonal quality of which it is capable seems to be in keeping with the mood and style of the music. Such moments cannot be identified with any one period. The soft pedal may be used in the music of Bach, giving that immediate change of sonority which is required in contrasting sections. Or its atmospheric effect may be required in passages from the music of the impressionistic composers, such as Ravel or Debussy. Needless to say, the soft pedal is held down *throughout* the passage selected and has no bearing on the sustaining pedal, which may or may not be used at the same time.

Many students make the mistake, when playing 'una corda' passages, of trying to use a touch below the normal level of sound. It must be realized, however, that a combination of soft pedal and flimsy fingers will render the best of instruments incapable of producing any singing tone, and that the pressure of the fingers must be as definite, and the tonal nuance as sensitive, as in all other music.

The student who wishes to use the pedals as a means of enhancing his performance must at all times pedal objectively. He should hear within himself the desired results and set the machinery into motion which will produce them. Nor is this all. If he contemplates playing in public he will need to know a little about acoustics, for these can play strange tricks with the sound. Let us say, as a rough guide, that in a hall where there is too much resonance—in some cases even an echo—the dampers must stay longer on the strings (the foot off the pedal) than usual. On the other hand, in a room which has hangings or curtains which tend to mop up the sound, the pedal can be held down for longer than usual. In addition a hall, which at the time of rehearsal was bare and empty and which seemed full of echo, will be far less resonant when, at the eventual performance, it is filled with people. Thus the performer needs a quick and sensitive criticism of sound and effect so that the final decision in the more subtle points of pedalling is 'of the moment', and the final court of appeal *the ear*.

THE PHRASE

Most books on piano-playing include a section devoted to phrasing, and though no chapter of this book bears such a heading, it has in fact been the underlying theme behind much that I have written. Good phrasing implies artistic and intelligent use of legato, staccato, accent, pause, and slur, a sense of balance between varying parts, a feeling for tonal nuance, a sensitive judgement of tempo and rhythmic variation, and an appreciation of the effects of pedalling. All these components are a part of the whole phrase, and on them its musical outline depends.

The instinct to divide musical composition into phrases is a natural one and as essential to the whole as punctuation is to speech. Our first subconscious realization of phrase-length was when we chanted the nursery rhymes of childhood, and quite young children, after a simple explanation, can tell how many phrases are contained in a short piece of music, *provided* it is played in such a way that the punctuation is made clear to them. We would, of course, first use music in which the phrases were equally balanced, for, as usual, the rule should be learnt before the exceptions. We would say, then, that a balanced musical sentence must have at least two phrases—these are spoken of as an 'announcing phrase' and an 'answering' (or 'responsive') phrase. The phrase is terminated by a cadence, and tonal nuance at phrase endings is determined by the type of cadence which occurs. For example, an imperfect cadence, especially when the 6/4 5/3 progression is used, indicates a tonal fading at the phrase end, whereas a perfect cadence implies a more definite approach to the final tonic.

Ex. 194.

Mendelssohn

This is just a simple illustration by way of a guide to the basic relationship of tonal control to phrasing. Many other aspects of rhythmic structure may have to be taken into consideration.

Phrase endings are usually indicated (in performance) by a slight break in the continuity of the sound, *but there must be no halt in the rhythmic flow*. This break is a natural one and should not give the impression of being deliberately imposed on the music—indeed, it may be likened to the breath taken by a singer or speaker. Where phrase endings occur, the moment and manner in which the final note is released depend on the style and character of the music. If the final note is followed by a rest, the moment of silence will, of course, be longer, but its length is also conditioned by other significant aspects of the musical structure, such as slur, staccato, accent, and so on. It will also be apparent that the break is likely to be more pronounced at the end of a complete sentence than after an announcing phrase. Perhaps it will interest the reader to turn to Exx. 42, 55, 72, 104, 146, 193, and 196, which contain a number of phrases each needing an individual approach to the manner in which they are terminated.

It must not be thought, however, that the significance of the phrase depends only on the performance of the *final* note. It is even more important for the phrase to be conveyed to the listener as having an individuality and shapeliness, and these depend on its structure, rhythmic, harmonic, and melodic. Indeed, there may be moments where a break between one phrase and another seems to be out of place. These moments occur in music which contains a flowing melodic line and which requires a sustained and cantabile touch. In such song-like melodies it is often better not to make a break between two related phrases, the first phrase-ending being indicated only by a tonal inflection. This is analogous with my suggestion regarding the slur in Ex. 46. The following may illustrate my meaning:

Ex. 195.

In the above I would also suggest that legato pedalling is used and that the dampers are not returned to the strings long enough to make a break in the sound between the two phrases. Though this may appear to contradict my earlier remarks about phrasing and pedalling (see page 104), here I am only referring to one short section; later in the piece there will still be a need for some kind of break, however short.

In contrast to a continuous legato we get the phrase which contains only staccato notes. About this Sidney Harrison says: 'The sense of *grouping notes in phrases* must be maintained in pieces that are so full of staccatos as not to allow for any slurring' [1] (the italics are mine). To this I need add nothing, except to point out that such phrases should have as much individuality and shapeliness as those which are legato.

In determining the shape of a phrase the first consideration is its point of climax. This point is often found to be on a strong beat towards the end of the phrase, but this is by no means the only possibility, for the climax may be felt on the first note, the last note, or half-way through a phrase. It will usually be found, however, that related phrases have the same shape. Thus, if the first phrase of a piece begins with an anacrusis and has its climax on the last strong beat, the second phrase and probably all others in the section will follow the same pattern. Freedom of phrase length is, however, becoming a characteristic of contemporary writing, and no inflexible rule can be made.

The problems become more complex when overlapping phrases appear, when either one phrase begins at the exact beat on which another terminates, or a new voice enters midway through the phrase of another. We can compare such things with the 'round' in which each group of singers is intent on one part, to which they give individual shape and climax. Thus the pianist has to appreciate the phrase shape and climax of each voice, so that he can clarify them in his performance and yet present the music as a complete and interblended whole. In this he needs the independence of tonal control, about which I spoke at some length in an earlier chapter.

Because we can only convey what we ourselves understand it will follow that analysis of phrasing and form should be part of the preparation of a work. Any pianist who has not realized this cannot be a complete musician and is unlikely to give a balanced performance. The study of musical form is a fascinating one and many excellent books can be got on the subject. Of these one of the most comprehensive is

[1] *Pianoforte Technique.*

Musical Form by Stewart Macpherson (Joseph Williams). From every point of view, whether professional or amateur, such a study can only be rewarding, and will open out fresh fields of interest and understanding to the concert-goer as well as the performer.

CONTINUITY

When all is said and done, when the music has been analysed, studied, and practised to the last demisemiquaver, a complete whole should emerge—a continuous thought—and this cannot be conveyed to the listener unless it is clear in the mind of the performer. All practising must be with this end in view, and the student needs to be able to 'think through' a work while he is still struggling with the notes of the first page. I therefore see no reason why he should not occasionally 'rough his way' through the music to find out the direction in which he is travelling, or simply play the melodic line throughout, if the music lends itself to this kind of exploration. Such a mental picture becomes increasingly important if the work to be studied is of any length, and a tremendous amount can be learnt from listening to broadcasts or recordings. Owners of tape recorders should find it rewarding to record and compare the interpretations of various artists, thus avoiding the only danger attendant on listening constantly to one performance—that of parrot-like imitation (see also page 71).

In discussing so many of the details which go towards a good performance I sincerely hope that my readers do not feel like the small boy who took his father's watch to pieces and found he could not put it together again! But, like the watch, successful performance and interpretation depend on perfection in so many small things.

As a piano teacher I almost feel that my pupils have written this book for me, because during their lessons I have been in the habit of jotting down any point which might form part of its subject-matter. But while most of these ideas have fitted into the various chapters, I still find myself left with a heterogeneous collection of facts which appear to have little relationship with each other and yet which I am determined to squeeze into the book somehow! After much thought, however, and perhaps a little 'wishful thinking', I have decided that they have one thing in common, and that is an effect upon the continuity of the whole.

It seems best to introduce each under a separate heading.

Fingering

Suitable choice of fingering is an essential to good performance, and one of the chief reasons for lack of fluency is thoughtless fingering (see Exx. 108 and 109). The foundations of good fingering habits are laid in the earlier lessons, and any student who has not a clear idea on these should read one of the many treatises available.[1] I myself dealt with the subject in some detail in *The Young Pianist*.

Many passages need careful finger-planning, and no student need be above writing in an occasional figure as a guide. When the fingering of a passage has been decided it should be adhered to on every occasion. In this way the fingers learn the notes by muscular habit, and the mind is free to attend to the details of interpretation. If the fingering is not planned, or is constantly changed, the feeling of safety is lost, resulting in unevenness of tone and rhythm and loss of continuity.

Slow Practice

All wise pianists practise slowly, indeed it is a vital factor in the overcoming of technical difficulties and in laying a safe foundation for the performance of quick passages. However well the piece is known, and at all grades and stages, a return to slow practice will help to ensure finger control under the stress of public performance.

It must be acknowledged, however, that intelligent slow

[1] I suggest *Pianoforte Fingering*, Thomas B. Knott (O.U.P.).

practice is quite different from monotonous slow practice. The section or phrase being practised should be as alive in its conception as it would be at the original speed. If we look at a small picture through a magnifying glass, the detail becomes *more* apparent, leading to an increased appreciation of the whole. Similarly, in slow practice it is better to exaggerate dynamics than to omit them. This focuses our mind on what we are doing and ensures that concentration is not lost.

Practising in Sections

It is often necessary to take one figure or section for special practice: this has to be repeated many times before the difficulties have been mastered. Such a process may take days or even weeks, by which time the relationship of the section with the whole is almost non-existent. To avoid this isolation the passage should be 'put back' into its context so that it may become 'familiar with its surroundings'. I have already mentioned that an occasional performance of the whole piece, even if somewhat roughed in in places, helps the student to have a complete picture of the whole. Similarly, after such a section has had its daily dose of technical practice, the student should play from the beginning of the piece or movement, neither stopping nor slowing down when the difficulties are reached. Though it may not yet be possible to get in all the notes, the passage in question can be outlined, either in melody or rhythmic pattern, so that it becomes part of the whole. Some may even find that they have an urge to sing their way through their difficulties, and this is an excellent idea, for it shows that the musical whole is already in their minds.

If the figure singled out for special practice is short—perhaps only one or two bars—incorporate it first of all in the phrase. Often I have heard my pupils after stumbling over a bar return to 'the beginning of the line' or 'the beginning of the page', or even 'the beginning of the bar'! How often they

fail to realize that I would prefer them to start at 'the beginning of the phrase'! Here we are back once again on the
necessity for appreciating phrase length in practice as well as
performance.

Silences

There is a tendency among pianists to treat a silence as a
kind of 'vacuum in sound' rather than as part of the continuity of the whole. A good ensemble player, practising a new
work for the first time and having several bars of rest, will not
consider that he knows his own part until he has found out
what everybody else does during those bars, after which he is
able to 'think through' his silences. Similarly, to the vocalist
the song *should* start at the beginning of the prelude and finish
at the end of the postlude.

There is, of course, a big difference between such silences
and those in solo piano works, but the analogy lies in the
necessity, in all cases, for continuous musical thought. In
piano music a silence *is* a silence, and yet it is part of the
music. Throughout its duration the pulse is still alive, and
demands absolute continuity of thought on the part of the
performer.

Silences may be divided into two categories—those within
a phrase or section which carry the ear onwards to the next
sound, and those more significant moments which precede a
change of tempo or mood. In both it is important to realize
that an exact moment of silence must be as accurately timed
as an exact moment of sound.

Normally the sound ceases on the beat on which the rest is
written, but this may be very slightly qualified if the rest is
preceded by a staccato note or slur. The manner of striking
and releasing the preceding note therefore effects the quality
of the silence.

Let us look at a few bars from the Chopin Scherzo in B♭
minor. The first two silences are exact—as though the sound
had been 'cut off with a knife' on the third beat. The third

silence following the *fz* staccato note almost hits us in the ear
with its abruptness:

Ex. 196.

In contrast there can be the silence that steals upon the ear
almost imperceptibly (see Ex. 42 on page 23), or the brief
pause in a series of whispered utterances:

Ex. 197.

It is evident that a rest in the score does not always denote
complete silence: this has been discussed in the section on
pedalling. The use or misuse of the pedal can, however, add
to or mar the effect where a silence is indicated. Abrupt
silences are made more effective by the precision of its release
(see Ex. 196), and others may be made ineffective if the
sound is allowed to continue, through indeterminate or care-
less pedalling.

I need hardly add that the beats contained within a silence
must be counted as exactly as the beats of any note value.
This may seem very elementary advice to students in the
more advanced grades, but I have often heard silences
cut short in bars 3 and 4 of the following, and similar
passages:

Ex. 198.

The closing bars of a work, or movement, may contain a long ritenuto in which rests are also included: in these places the rests are felt within the gradually slowing tempo, the whole process continuing as smoothly as if the silences were replaced by sounds.

The silence which precedes a change of mood or key may be considered as a moment of preparation or of 'looking forward'. If the reader will experiment with other works than those given here, I do not think he will ever find one that does not impel his inward ear forward to that which is to follow:

Thus, the thoughts of the performer moving forward towards that which is to come, he carries his audience across the void without imparting a feeling of momentary 'nothingness', each silence becoming a living and vital part of the whole.

Turning the pages

I wonder how many people realize that turning the pages should be practised as part of the performance, especially if the work is to be played from the music on some special occasion. Bad turns, even during practice, may lead to a habitual rhythmic hitch which becomes so ingrained that the eventual co-operation of a 'turner over' fails to save the situation. Phrase length is always the first consideration, and, even though the student may feel he cannot memorize a whole piece, surely it would be worth the effort to memorize a few bars for the sake of continuity. There is often a phrase ending just before or just after the turning place, or at a point in which only one hand is not fully occupied. In most instances it is better to keep the pulse going and miss out a few notes in an accompanying part than to stop the rhythmic impulse of the music. One of the most astonishing bits of turning over I ever heard happened at a Festival class in which the set piece was a Chopin Waltz. In some editions of this Waltz the turn comes at the end of the first section, with three notes of the next section printed before the turn.

We were treated to this:

Ex. 201.

long pause to turn over, then:

Ex. 201a.

etc.

Turns, therefore, must be thought out, rehearsed, and made safe unless the student can memorize the work very quickly. There will always be moments when the turn really is impossible; many of the fugues of Bach keep both hands occupied throughout, and not a note can be spared without breaking the thread of one or other voice. There is little advice I can offer here beyond urging the pianist who intends to play in public either to memorize the work or to make sure that someone is prepared to turn over. When the music-stand is large enough, and in a work that does not occupy more than four pages, I have known students take *two* copies and place them side by side! If this works, all well and good: anything is worth trying that allows the musical line to continue unbroken.

Ornaments

The word 'ornament' in its everyday use implies an addition or embellishment to the main structure which, though it is intended to add charm or attractiveness, does not in any way alter the basic design. The *musical* ornament, however, has more importance than this. In the early days of keyboard writing, when the instruments provided little or no means of sustaining the sound, ornaments were often added to increase the resonance of the longer note values. But with Bach, and following on from him, the ornament becomes an integral part of the whole, frequently filling in and completing the melody or harmony.

Since the ornament is not outside the structure but within it, it should take its mood and tonal level from the music in which it is embodied, and thus should in no way disturb the rhythmic impulse of the music. Many students, however, on seeing notes of ornamentation show signs of what might be called 'rhythmic hysteria'—thus we get an unexpected bulge in the tone, or a hiatus in the rhythmic progression which completely destroys the continuity of the whole.

It must be appreciated, then, that though the rudimentary rules of ornamentation lay down that a trill or a turn at a certain tempo must contain so many semiquavers or demi-semiquavers, ultimately the number of notes to be played has to depend on the context, or on the ability of the performer to negotiate the technical difficulties presented! In trills the speed of the reiterated notes may have to be modified to suit a technique that is not quite adequate. Certain well-known classics, ideal as an introduction to the more advanced works of the various composers, contain trills or other ornaments which add considerably to their technical difficulty. Among these is the first movement of Mozart's Sonata in C, K. 545. This charming work is often attempted by young pianists who have neither the musical understanding nor the technical qualifications to give it a performance. Thus one hears it played far too slowly or else at a variety of speeds through-out. There are, of course, young students who get very near to giving a performance of this music, but even they are usually unable to maintain the rhythmic impulse when they reach the trill bars at the end of each section. Here the rhythm either loses its impetus or disintegrates completely while the pianist laboriously 'gets in' every note of the trill. A far more satisfactory solution, and one that is quite in keeping with the music, is to modify the trill, reducing the speed of the notes from demisemiquavers to semi-quavers. In this way every note of the left hand remains rhythmically correct and the final cadence is clearly heard. Thus:

Ex. 202.

is realized as:

Ex. 202a.

Such modifications also apply to shorter trills coming at cadence points. If the tempo is fast, the trill is, in any case, played as a turn of five notes, but even at a slow tempo a simple five-note turn would be more acceptable than a 'scrambled' trill. Thus, the trill in the following:

Ex. 203.

could well be played in this way:

Ex. 203a

The turn (or the trill which implies a turn) must be played with complete clarity. If this cannot be achieved with five notes then it is better to play only four. Thus a student who adopts a suitably fast tempo for these opening bars:

Ex. 204.

may need to reduce the number of notes in the succeeding phrase. Thus:

is reduced from

to

Similarly, turns following a dotted note which should according to the rule be delayed, may often be played *on* the beat to fit in with a moving part. For example, the turn in the following:

though interpreted in many footnotes as:

could well be played as:

Ex. 206b.

Indeed, many experienced pianists prefer this interpretation
as more in keeping with the mood of the music.

Mordents are also frequently hurried or played indis-
tinctly, especially against other moving voices in contrapuntal music. In such music the initial note comes *on* the
beat, and performance will become much easier and more
correct if an exact time relationship is established between
such ornaments and the other parts. This passage will illustrate:

Ex.207.
Bach

can be realized as:

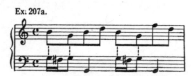

Ex. 207a.

One further example shows how easily the shake should be
made to fit into the flowing accompaniment in the Allemande
from the French Suite in G:

Ex.208.
Bach

realized:

Ex. 208a.

It will, I hope, be appreciated that this is not a treatise on the *reading* of ornaments. Such an important subject is one for the specialist to handle, though it should be studied as an integral part of every musician's training. Any detailed study is far beyond the scope of a book such as this, but the point that I wish to make here is the necessity of keeping a sense of proportion when playing figures of ornamentation. Many pianists, who are far above the grade to which this section may appear to be addressed, would do well to modify their trills and turns, so as not to give the impression of scramble. The rule should always be: 'Listen to the basic pulse, and make sure that the ornaments do not detract in any way from its life and impetus'.

The virtuoso pianist will have learnt to trill with both speed and strength, but he does not allow every trill to hit us in the ear like an alarm clock. Those embodied in a slow-moving music are not intended to be 'brilliant', but take their speed and tonal level from the mood and structure of the whole.

Mannerisms

It is an undisputed fact that most concert-goers like to watch the soloist: indeed, this is borne out by the number of people who book early to make sure of having a seat on the keyboard side. Television brings the audience almost too close to the pianist at times, and, though I prefer sound radio, I still find the attraction of the eye irresistible if I 'look in' on a concert. Here we are transported from side to side of the piano with breath-taking speed, and if I shut my eyes, in an effort to concentrate only on the sound, it is not very long before the urge to open them again finds me poised in mid-air, looking down on the stage from a new angle. On the whole I prefer the safety of my seat on the keyboard side, from which too I must admit I like to listen *and look*!

For the 'lookers', then, there must be something that will enhance or detract from a performance, though the discerning ear *should* qualify any visual impression made. What exactly is it that we are looking for? Naturally attractiveness or good looks do not go unnoticed, and a beautiful gown may be commented on by the female members of the audience! But these things are mere side issues for those who have taken the trouble to buy their seats on the keyboard side. We go to see 'how it is done'—to watch the hands, the fingers, and the arms, and those other movements which are part of the personal style of the pianist. Some pianists move very little when they play, others seem unable to play a single note without a complete bodily movement; yet in both categories we hear pianists of the highest order.

From the point of view of a teacher I would rather deal with the pupil who appears to me to move too much than with one who sits like a ramrod and whose whole appearance, including her facial expression, seems to have no connection with what her hands and fingers are doing. It is usually possible for the teacher to check over-emphasis of bodily movement, but no movement that is not spontaneous can be imposed.

Where is all this leading? What has it to do with continuity? I would say that movements at the keyboard may be classified into two groups—in the first are those arm and hand movements necessary for the job in hand, combined with an unconscious bodily movement impelled by the rhythmic urge of the music. In the second are extraneous movements which appear to have no bearing on the music and which detract from the visual concept of continuity. These imposed movements are often a form of 'showmanship' and as such are completely undesirable. A pupil who came to me once swayed so violently that it made me feel quite seasick to look at her. She told me (some time later) that she had been *taught* to do this as one of the necessary tricks of pianism.

Awkward mannerisms may be unconscious, and they tend to grow if we are not told about them. Even the virtuoso pianist is not free of such things, and he is at a disadvantage if none of his friends dare criticize.

So there will always be pianists who are more suitable for radio than television, and if any of my readers have an ambition to appear on the platform or television screen it would be worth inviting the criticism of the more honest of their friends, so that unwanted mannerisms shall not detract from their performance.

Concentration, Memory, and Nerves

Piano-playing, like every other art, requires concentration. But the average person has the greatest difficulty in focusing the mind for more than a few minutes at a time. The artist who reaches the top does so by a self-discipline and single-mindedness that can only be achieved through perseverance and determination. It has often been said that the student who practises for half an hour with his mind fixed on the work will achieve more than he who practises for two hours with his thoughts on other things. If this is true in general it is doubly true when it comes to memorizing. Allowing for the fact that some have a naturally better memory than others, it may still be said that the pianist who says he cannot memorize has given in far too easily.

Memory can only be reliable when the music is in the mind as well as in the fingers. The soloist who relies on muscular memory will come to grief directly he begins wondering what the next note is. So much has been said and written about nerves and memory that I feel it would be superfluous to say it again, but I would stress that the music which has been studied and learnt with complete concentration is more likely to have impressed itself on the mind, than if the fingers have been allowed to 'take over' during certain sections of practice.

It is recognized that a performance from memory makes a better visual impression on the audience than one with the music. I do not say *from* the music, because there is a vast difference between having a copy there for occasional reference, and being so unsure that the eyes have to be fixed on the music throughout. But even when the work *has* been well-prepared a lurking anxiety over one ticklish spot can easily detract from the performance. Frank Merrick sums up the relative advantages and disadvantages of playing from memory by suggesting that the final decision should be the quality of the performance that can be offered with or without the music.[1] I would, however, qualify this by suggesting that performance from memory should be the *aim* of all aspiring pianists and that no one should consider he knows a work really well until he can at least play it from memory at home.

Nerves at the time of performance are often the cause of unexpected memory slips, and the constant cry is: 'How can I cure myself of nerves?' The answer is that no one can; nerves are part of our physical make-up and we might as well try to 'cure' ourselves of seeing, hearing, or feeling. The musician is said, like members of many other professions connected with the arts, to be more prone to nervous excitement than the more phlegmatic of his friends. Accidents will surely happen, especially with the young and inexperienced artist, but an audience is always sympathetic and it is rare for a sincere and well-prepared pianist to come completely to grief.

Any musician who is keyed up before a concert will experience a feeling of nervous excitement and anticipation. Nor must the artist who is making his debut expect that this will disappear as the years go by. The more experienced the pianist the more he feels a sense of responsibility—to the composer, to the audience, to other members of an orchestra or ensemble.

[1] *Practising the Piano* (Rockliffe).

Having acknowledged the *existence* of nerves, the inexperienced artist must start by eliminating the conditions
which allow them to take the upper hand. In the main these
are:

1. Not knowing the work sufficiently well to stand the
extra strain of public performance.
2. Being unaccustomed to playing before an audience.
3. Lack of complete concentration at the time of performance.

The first of these three can only be the result of insufficient
preparation. Before playing in public the soloist needs to
know the music so well that he could start at any given bar
and continue from there. The mind must be completely
familiar with the harmonic and structural design and the
fingers must have attained the muscular habit by which technical perfection is achieved. Many of the finest pianists—or
indeed soloists in any musical field—have been known to
study certain works for many years before considering they
were ready to play them in public. Even at smaller and more
informal concerts a piece must be far better known than
many students realize if it is to come unscathed through the
ordeal.

The second condition—being unaccustomed to playing
before an audience—can only be overcome if the student
finds some way of collecting an audience on which to re-
hearse! No opportunity to play in public should be missed.
Often valuable experience is lost through hesitation or diffi-
dence. Neither should any aspiring pianist be above playing
in a show which he does not consider sufficiently highbrow.
It would be easy to give a list of today's top-ranking pianists
who started their careers playing for concert parties, or as an
accompaniment to the conversation of the guests of Lady X.
Anything that gives experience is worth trying, and no re-
quest to play should ever be refused. If necessary the pianist

will have to implore or even bribe his friends to come and listen to him!

My third condition is: 'Lack of complete concentration at the time of performance.' 'Surely', it will be said, 'no one would attempt to play in public without thinking what he is doing.' There is, however, a way of thinking in which one small part of the mind wanders from our control. 'I wonder if the family managed to get here in time'—'Who was that sitting in the front row? I know the face quite well', etc., etc. These and other little thoughts come crowding in just before we begin to play, and, though we switch our minds back to the job in hand the moment we *start* playing, the mind is, as it were, one move behind, and does not always completely catch up with the single mindedness which is essential to complete concentration.

Few concert artists like to carry on any kind of conversation immediately before a performance (*or* during the interval). To them the time of concentration starts *before* they appear on the platform. Anyone who has noticed the absorption of many soloists during the orchestral part of a piano concerto will realize how completely he or she has already become identified with the music. The soloist who fidgets and fiddles or gazes round at the audience during these times is much less likely to settle down to a performance of any real worth.

Only a small proportion of those who study the piano do so with the object of becoming concert pianists and a smaller proportion still reach the heights to which they aspire. Yet, to all, the ability to concentrate becomes the most valuable of attainments. Whether it be in study, teaching, or performance, the work will be better done and the results far more satisfying.

Sight-reading

Natural brilliance in sight-reading is a heaven-sent gift: the people who have this gift will tell you that they never remem-

ber a time when reading the music presented any difficulty.
I have experienced a sense of wonder, and even awe, when a
seven-year-old pupil seemed able to read music, and even
convey some of its meaning, before I had taught her all the
notes.

Let the average pianist take heart, however, for he can become a good sight-reader if he is prepared to give sufficient
time to practising this much-neglected art. In this the
amateur often outstrips the professional, for his music-making
is frequently a form of exploration of the vast amount of
musical literature at his disposal. Those who meet together
to play duets or to take part in any form of musical ensemble
are far more likely to read well than those who never leave
the solo field of music-making. Ensemble-playing compels
the individual to maintain continuity, whereas the solo sight-
reader often ambles along in his own time, pausing to puzzle
out a note here and there, and finishing triumphantly 'without having made any mistakes'. In actual fact, loss of continuity is the biggest mistake of all. I have always been so
anxious to impress this on my pupils that one of them re-
ceived this comment from a festival adjudicator: 'I have
never heard anyone play so many wrong notes so beautifully,
you almost convinced me that you were right!' This particular pupil had a very poor visual perception, though her sense
of performance was above the average. In tackling her reading in this way it improved steadily, though it would never
have become outstanding. She did, at least, manage to gain
pass marks for Sight-reading in her Diploma Examination,
though I am sure she must have played a lot of wrong notes!

To be a good sight-reader is a wonderful thing, well worth
the effort of cultivation. It opens up the way to endless
musical discoveries and will give as much pleasure to the
ordinary average pianist as is felt by the virtuoso who has
stormed the heights of technical achievement.

CONCLUSION

Why do we play the piano? It must surely be because we like it, for having reached the years of discretion it can no longer be 'because Mummy wants me to!' We have now realized that we ourselves want to go on, and that whatever our grade or stage there is always more to learn.

Piano-playing is intended in the first place to be a pleasure, but if it is to become our profession, either as teacher or as performer, it cannot just be left at that. The performer carries the responsibility of becoming the medium for the transference of musical thought, and the teacher's responsibility lies in equipping the pupil to do so.

If, therefore, I have made the art of piano-playing appear to be a very serious business, it is only that, in the end, the pleasure derived from it may be increased by a deeper understanding of the problems involved and a wider appreciation of the possibilities of the instrument.

What of the amateur—he who plays entirely for his own pleasure? I hope that he, too, will feel that it is worth his while going a little below the surface and considering such problems as tonal fading, rhythmic variation, or sympathetic vibration, where understanding can add so much to his playing. It appears to me that an appreciation of such things can only be rewarding. The professional pianist seldom plays 'just for pleasure', and those who treat music-making as a pastime may indeed be said to have the germ of music within their souls. For these people I would like to quote from an article by Martin Cooper, which appeared in the *Daily Telegraph* in April 1958:

'Meanwhile the piano remains the ideal instrument for the ordinary amateur music lover, not only for the sake of its incomparable literature (which no other solo instrument can faintly rival) but because it provides the natural introduction to the whole field of music, and, by its means, even quite a humble performer can become acquainted with the operatic and symphonic repertory.'

It may be said that few of my readers will ever mount the concert platform as virtuoso performers; indeed, what I have said will only serve to set their feet upon the lowest rung of the ladder. But if I have been able to pass on, however inadequately, thoughts that are of interest to the aspiring soloist, then I shall indeed be pleased.

It is my hope that all who have read this book, whether they be teachers, students, professionals, or amateurs, will have found at least one idea to give them a fresh interest and a measure of encouragement.

INDEX